Miracle at the Forks

PETER C. NEWMAN | ALLAN LEVINE

MIRACLE AT THE FORKS

The Museum That Dares Make a Difference

THE CANADIAN MUSEUM
FOR HUMAN RIGHTS

Figure.1
Vancouver / Berkeley

Cataloguing data available from Library and Archives Canada
ISBN 978-1-927958-21-6 (hbk.)

Editing by Sarah Brohman
Copy editing by Judy Phillips
Design by Jessica Sullivan
Cover photograph by Aaron Cohen
Slipcase photographs by Patrick Coulie

Printed and bound in Canada by Friesens
Distributed in the U.S. by Publishers Group West

Figure 1 Publishing Inc.
Vancouver, BC Canada
www.figure1pub.com

Dedicated to the memory of Israel Asper, OC, OM, LL.D. (1932–2003) and Ruth "Babs" Asper (1933–2011), whose imagination, vision, dedication, and perseverance transformed the Canadian Museum for Human Rights from a dream to a reality.

And to the more than 7,800 generous donors and hundreds of supporters who have worked tirelessly to ensure that the dream did not die.

FOREWORD

WE WOULD LIKE to thank our late chair of the Asper Foundation, Ruth (Babs) Asper, who thought this story contained many lessons to be learned of perseverance and unwavering optimism and who encouraged the publication of this book. Our appreciation goes to her and to our other trustees, David Asper, Leonard Asper, and Richard Leipsic, for believing in us along this long journey that was fraught with many risks. We applaud the trustees for committing over $20 million to the project and taking on all the development costs for the eight years before the museum was formally established as a national institution.

We thank the Right Honourable Stephen Harper, who believed that we needed a national project, the first outside the capital region, which would stand as a symbol of Canada's commitment to freedom, democracy, human rights, and the rule of law. We owe the creation of Canada's fifth national museum to him. We also thank the Right Honourable Jean Chrétien for his pivotal support in the beginning and for giving us the opportunity to build on this idea, and the Right Honourable Paul Martin for taking us to the next level of support and encouragement. To all the ministers of Western Economic Diversification and Canadian Heritage and their staff, thank you for over a decade of tireless work, for believing in this project, and for helping make it a reality.

To the premiers of Manitoba, Gary Doer and Greg Selinger, and Mayors Glen Murray and Sam Katz and their staff, who eagerly signed on to this important project, thank you for recognizing the importance in the museum and for investing the necessary funds required to make it happen.

To our small team at the Friends of the Canadian Museum of Human Rights, board members, campaign teams, and volunteers across the country, we and Canada owe you our greatest appreciation. To the many thousands of donors from across Canada, whether for the

$5 sent lovingly with an inspiring note or the many other millions donated, this is your museum. Thanks also to all the various communities that came together to speak with one voice in support of the museum.

To the chairs of the CMHR Board of Trustees, first Arni Thorsteinson and now Eric Hughes, and to the members of the board past and present, thank you for your leadership, courage, and commitment to ensure that all Canadians will regard this as an important investment in their future. And many thanks to Stuart Murray and his team, who have taken on one of the most complex and difficult challenges in museum making.

As we finish this long journey that started over fourteen years ago, we now take great pride in seeing the spectacularly designed Antoine Predock wonder and the brilliant exhibit design work of Ralph Appelbaum and his team as it unfolds.

Finally and most important, we reserve our deepest appreciation for our families—our spouses, Michael Paterson and Barbara Levy, and our children, Stephen and Jonathan Paterson, and Adam, Samuel, and Sarah Levy—who endured our many absences and who gave us the encouragement over the years to pursue this dream.

We hope that when you read this book and follow the journey, so brilliantly written by Peter C. Newman and Allan Levine, it will serve as an inspiration and acknowledgment that anything is possible when you have passion, persistence, and an outstanding team committed to excellence. As the late Israel Asper noted many times, "Here we are reaching for the stars . . . to create an international architectural icon, a symbol of Canada."

We hope and believe that we have delivered on this dream.

GAIL ASPER, O.C., O.M., LL.D.
President | The Asper Foundation

MOSES (MOE) LEVY
Executive Director | The Asper Foundation

INTRODUCTION

THE KEY TO reading this book is remaining open to discovery. It is designed to replicate the lively journey of a wanderer traversing the wilderness of the Red River's backcountry, and suddenly encountering a palace. The building has no recognizable shape, and seems to be wrapped in candy floss, but it draws the wandering visitor into its vertical embrace through a symbolic "pillar of fire" that pierces the prairie sky. Only at the last moment does the building reveal itself to be the world's first museum for human rights.

Standing among its mighty architectural roots and looking up, you are confronted by the visual impact of the structure's elephant-sized reality, located at the forks of two mighty rivers in the heart of Manitoba. Designed to astonish any visitor who expects to see the usual stuffy, square silhouette of a museum, its awesome dimensions hypnotize. This promises to be a unique institution for which there are no comparables. It is, quite simply, a dramatic architectural statement equal in originality to Australia's famed Sydney Opera House.

Its architecture expresses the commonality of mankind—a symbolic apparition of ice, clouds, and stone set squarely in a place where Aboriginals have walked, talked, and traded for an estimated six thousand years.

Journalist Dan Lett accurately summed up the museum's key puzzle in the *Winnipeg Free Press* on December 24, 2011, by asking, "Whenever it finally opens, will one of the museum's displays be as compelling as the story of how it got built?" Most people won't have a problem agreeing with Lett's observation.

The lofty mission of the Canadian Museum for Human Rights (CMHR) is to place the issue of human rights under pressure—their past (to learn lessons); their present (to monitor progress); and their future (to resolve tensions between reform and inaction). According to its guiding principles, the CMHR also

> aspires to offer its visitors an
> inspiring encounter with human
> rights while exceeding Canadians'

top The museum pierces the prairie sky and can be seen far and wide across the city.

above Israel and Babs Asper each devoted the last years of their lives to the dream of the CMHR.

expectations for balance, transparency, sound business practices and meaningful public consultation; fosters an appreciation for the importance of human rights, spurs informed dialogue and invites participants to identify the contemporary relevance of past and present human rights events, both at home and abroad; the museum exemplifies Canadians' commitment to freedom and democracy and aims to ignite an informed, ever-evolving global conversation; provides a safe and engaging space to cultivate respect, gratitude, understanding and ongoing improvement of this human rights inheritance … [and] connects its visitors with opportunities to explore the global development of human rights concepts and Canada's important role within it.

Such is the narrative arc of this amazing undertaking: how to discover and disseminate the notion of living and acting according to

universal rules that apply to people of all cultures, languages, and religions.

The unique structure fulfills the dreams and ambitions of its originator, the late Winnipeg-based billionaire and media mogul Israel "Izzy" Asper and his family: Babs, Gail, David, and Leonard Asper. Conscious of how the museum would best achieve its essential mission, they happily passed the torch to the federal government in 2007 so that the museum's human rights mandate would be protected. Equally relevant are the fulfilled aspirations of the CMHR's 7,800 patrons and volunteers who donated the $146 million (and still counting) required to make this dream come true. Their dedication to the cause of human rights goes beyond rhetoric.

In the spring of 2003, the prospect of raising the enormous amount of funds required for such a gargantuan project seemed as improbable and intimidating as trying to scale Mount Everest on a dinner date. And it was. What it required was a "miracle at the Forks." A quarter of a million visitors are expected to view the museum in its opening year. But as the message that this is a must-see and must-tour spectacle spreads by word of mouth, it is certain that even more Canadians will want to satisfy their curiosity.

To the surprise of its worried planners and builders, and to the disappointment of its detractors, something remarkable has taken place: the museum lives. It was a brave and daring idea that some deemed far too risky to be Canadian. And yet it has materialized, contradicting the dire prognostications of some very sensible people.

What makes the CMHR so fascinating—and the main reason it deserves a book—is that it is a museum like no other; its existence demands we pay attention to its mission: to make humanity more amenable to human rights and civil liberties.

It is no accident that the museum's physical environment and superior acoustics echo

4

majesty and gravitas. Its architecture is stunning, but its stature will be judged by how effectively its occupants and visitors formulate and transmit the urgent need to improve people's individual and collective human rights. Even more adventurous and original in its unusual design than the spectacular Canadian Museum of History (formerly known as the Canadian Museum of Civilization) built in 1989 in Hull, across the Ottawa River from the nation's capital, the CMHR in Winnipeg has pioneered the groundbreaking notion of building national museums outside Canada's National Capital Region. The CMHR's exhibits include historical objects that imaginatively reconstruct the harsh realities of human rights abuses throughout history. The interactive displays set the mood, provide the context, and ably demonstrate the dilemma that the concepts of universal human rights have developed out of negative freedoms—as in the sense that people sought freedom *from* oppression in their

physical, economic, political, and spiritual lives. The world bursts with fault lines in the arena of human rights that deserve to be resolved and eliminated. The CMHR rightly emphasizes that it is not enough simply to be free *from* oppression; we must also be free *to* live, to work, to worship, and we must respect the rights of others to do so as well.

THE CANADIAN Museum for Human Rights owes its existence primarily to Prime Minister Stephen Harper. It was he who pledged that the Canadian government would provide the project's annual operating funding in perpetuity, funding that allowed the CMHR to fly its course. Although Asper and Harper never met in person to discuss the project, Asper's lieutenants—daughter Gail, wife Babs, sons David and Leonard, and his chief of staff, Moses (Moe) Levy—successfully carried the burdens of advocacy. Gail and Moe's extraordinary campaign was one of the most successful Canadian

top Architect Antoine Predock's
original sketch of the CMHR.

above, overleaf The CMHR is designed
to astonish any visitor.

fundraisers ever. But their own contributions went beyond the financial, and they proved to doubters that Canadians appreciated the need for this kind of museum.

Izzy Asper's operatives didn't just lobby Ottawa; their mission was to obliterate the government's option of denial. Moe Levy was in the capital so often that he stayed in just about every one of the Château Laurier hotel's 429 rooms. The rumour whispered in Ottawa's corridors of power among the bureaucrats who counted was that if Gail and Moe had eased up, the project might have been expedited. That rumour wasn't true, but they did go so often that even the most soft-hearted bureaucrats glanced heavenward in exasperation whenever they appeared. Driven advocates they had to be, as they faced long odds: three prime ministers, a serious recession, an entrenched bureaucratic culture, severe cutbacks in federal spending,

and an untested team pioneering an unprecedented public-private fiscal structure.

Asper died of a heart attack at the age of seventy-one in the autumn of 2003 just as the architectural competition for the CMHR's design was about to begin. It was his lieutenants who carried the struggle for most of the project, but Izzy was its visionary originator.

above Aerial view of the Canadian Museum for Human Rights at the Forks and the Esplanade Riel over the Red River, October 21, 2011.

01

REACHING FOR THE STARS

IT IS A PUZZLE, even in retrospect: Why did Israel "Izzy" Asper, a Jewish multi-billionaire who did it all and had everything he could ever want—including a manor in Palm Beach— expend precious energy and contribute more than $20 million to build a museum in Winnipeg, where the weather swings between winter and August? Housing permanent exhibits as well as scholars dedicated to the defence and definition of civil liberties, an institution of this style and class has never been attempted before—anywhere, anytime. One reason might be the difficulties posed by the mounting of exhibits of human rights, perhaps more challenging than throwing up the usual museum fare of dinosaurs from the Cretaceous era. And building a museum is not a cheap venture: the Canadian Museum for Human Rights (CMHR) cost $351 million at the latest count.

This unique quest followed standard Asper procedure. Driven by unrelenting self-determination that rivalled the monomaniacal zeal of Captain Ahab, Asper and his devoted co-conspirators spent a nerve-destroying decade on the project. It is easy to call this quest an obsession, but in the Asper catalogue, nearly everything he did was obsessive: collecting George Gershwin memorabilia, doggedly pursuing the establishment of a third Canadian television network, or quaffing yet another of his "prairie martinis" (double raw gin on ice).

The Friends were quick to point out that this was not just another of Asper's many diversions. The CMHR would be his legacy. Asper was well aware of the museum's significance—not as a personal memorial (it is now in the hands of the Canadian federal government)—but as an institution of learning and teaching, as well as the preserving, of human rights. It would fill essential gaps of knowledge while making the world a more civilized place. In retrospect, for Izzy Asper, the museum was more devotion than obsession.

IMPATIENT FROM the day he was born, Izzy Harold Asper arrived prematurely on August 11, 1932, in Minnedosa, a puppy bush settlement in rural Manitoba. He had two older siblings: a brother, Aubrey, born in 1929, and a sister, Hettie, born in 1930. Izzy recalled feeling insulted because his parents, Leon and Cecilia, did not immediately rush out to show him off in nearby Winnipeg. His refugee parents, originally from Odessa—Cecilia immigrated to Canada in 1921 with her parents, and Leon arrived in 1924— were classically trained musicians who travelled for work during the Depression. Leon was a violinist and conducted a string quartet in the Canadian Pacific Palliser Hotel in Calgary, Cecilia was an accomplished pianist, and they both played background music for silent films in movie theatres. When the talkies arrived in the early 1930s, the Aspers purchased Minnedosa's Lyric Theatre and turned it into a movie theatre. Leon acted as the projectionist, while Cecilia was the cashier, and eventually they built a

small movie chain. The family occupied a large house in Minnedosa that had no indoor plumbing. A self-sufficient man, Leon Asper imported kosher meat from Winnipeg in his unrefrigerated van; the meat was often rancid by the time it reached the dinner table.

Izzy did not enjoy a happy childhood as he tried to bridge his contemporary, mischievous reality with a strict old-school father who preached duty instead of joy. In the mornings before school, he would scrape chewing gum off the movie house seats with a penknife. Young Izzy tried escaping from home when he was only ten but was soon returned by a friendly constable.

After his fourteenth birthday, Izzy rode his bike eighteen miles each evening delivering films, and by the age of seventeen he had taken over the management of one of his parents' movie theatres. At the time, downtown Minnedosa consisted of the Patricia Café, owned by Tony Evans (a former wrestler); the elegant Tremont Hotel, a classy institution with a Sunday evening roast-beef special; and an ice cream parlour run by "Tubby" Anderson.

Although Izzy showed no particular promise in his youth, he accomplished enough for half a dozen lifetimes. But he never considered that he had met his potential. The museum was his last act, and he reached for the stars.

RIGHT FROM THE beginning of his life in Minnedosa, the home of only one other Jewish family (the Rykiss clan, who ran a dry goods store), Izzy Asper experienced vicious anti-Semitism, the long trail of which would haunt his personal life and his career. Izzy and Aubrey were frequent targets of hurtful rants from fellow students and suffered several beatings on their way to and from school.

During the 1930s, the climate of Winnipeg was riddled with anti-Semitism. Winnipeg's German Consulate was manned by two consuls, Heinrich Seelheim, from 1930 to 1937, who joined the Nazi Party in 1934, and Wilhelm Rodde, from 1937 to 1939, who already had been a member of the party for three years when he accepted the posting in Manitoba. Both actively supported Nazi policies and distributed anti-Jewish hate propaganda across the Prairies.

Winnipeg was also headquarters of the Canadian Nationalist Party, led by the professional Jew-baiter William Whittaker, who dressed in Nazi Party brown shirts and riding boots. In his racist tabloid, the *Canadian Nationalist,*

Whittaker reproduced the infamous forgery *The Protocols of the Elders of Zion,* which received much publicity a decade earlier when it had been the basis for dozens of defamatory articles in automobile magnate Henry Ford's newspaper, the *Dearborn Independent.* Whittaker lauded Hitler for "placing the Jew just where he belonged" and posted notices throughout the city labelling Jews "cowards" and the "Son of Satan." He was denounced in the editorial pages of the *Winnipeg Free Press* and by an assortment of local politicians, but this did nothing to stop him.

There were altercations and brief skirmishes between Whittaker's followers and young Jewish Winnipeggers, many of whom were members of the city's Anti-Fascist League's youth wing. In early June 1934, Whittaker announced plans for a large parade. On the day of the march, June 5, dozens of fascists and many more anti-fascists clashed in a bloody riot at Market Square. It was the worst violence in the city since the General Strike of 1919.

"Knives flashed in the fast waning sunlight, heavy clubs crashed against cap-protected skulls, and huge slabs of wood were torn from the stalls of the market gardeners and used as battering rams," the *Winnipeg Free Press* reported on June 6, 1934. "Badly outnumbered ... the brown shirted Nationalists suffered heavy losses." Appearing in court bruised and beaten, Whittaker, unrepentant to the end, declared that the riot was "the first battle in the cause of Gentile economic freedom." On the other hand,

11

adds Fred Narvey, then a twenty-one-year-old member of the Anti-Fascist League, it "was the first and last time that fascists tried to march in Winnipeg."

Anti-Semitism also found its way into the Faculty of Medicine at the University of Manitoba, which had a severe quota system from 1932 to 1944. Appearing before the 1944 provincial government committee hearing convened to investigate allegations about the quota system, the dean of medicine, Dr. Alvin Mathers, who had instituted the quota system, insisted that "certain nationalities" would never be accepted as doctors, so there was no point in training them, and he warned that the "University of Manitoba might become too Jewish." Following the provincial government investigation that substantiated the charges that the quota system indeed existed—Mathers and university officials had initially denied that it did—the university was compelled by the government to halt the practice immediately and insert into its regulations that henceforth "the selection [of Faculty of Medicine candidates] shall be made without regard to the racial origin or religion of the applicant."

When the Asper family moved to Winnipeg in 1946, Izzy became a Zionist and joined the labour Habonim organization, explaining that the left-wing girls enjoyed a much more bohemian approach to life than did those in the stern group of Young Judaea Zionists. He also went to B'nai Brith summer camp, where

he learned to swim, and even rescued the drowning Larry Zolf, future CBC gadfly, satirist, and well-informed commentator. Asper claimed not to remember the incident and vehemently denied that he considered throwing him back in. When not studying at the University of Manitoba, Izzy joined a teenage gang of a dozen muscle boys who would sneak into rich people's garages, lift up their cars, and set them down sideways so they couldn't be driven out.

It was in university that he met his future wife, Ruth Miriam "Babs" Bernstein. They courted, but Izzy was so busy with extracurricular activities they could only meet late at night. Babs's parents started referring to him as "Mister Coffee" because at about eleven each evening their daughter would announce, "I'm going for coffee" and head out to meet her beau. "We then started going out together more," Izzy recalled. "She owned the first long-playing record I'd ever seen, and it was Dave Brubeck doing 'Take Five.' That got to me. Here was a good-looking girl who understood this music and loved it, even owned the record. You can build on that!" On May 24, 1956, Brubeck was playing at the Black Hawk bar in San Francisco. In those days you couldn't travel with a girl across the border unless you were married, so Izzy and Babs tied the knot and got to see Brubeck live in concert.

Young Asper had a tough grind in law school, not with his studies but in getting to class. In

the second year, his attendance record didn't even rank as sporadic. "Law School was death warmed over," he recalled. "You had to have 80 percent attendance. In my second year, I had 12 percent, quit once and then got 'chucked' out. I couldn't take it. I remember putting my hand up and giving my version of the law and the prof would say, 'What's your name? Asper. Oh right, we know about you.' " Izzy was told that he wasn't there to say what the law ought to be, but to learn what it was. He did eventually graduate in law and was fortunate enough to be offered a tiny office on top of the local Bank of Nova Scotia vault on a pay-when-you-can basis. He boasted to his friends that he was sitting on a million dollars, but went for eight months without a client. ("I had no air conditioning—I kept the window open.")

In Winnipeg, he set up a primarily Jewish law firm that did so well he eventually decided to branch out and build a small distillery to produce various liquors strictly for export, which meant that he didn't have to carry inventory. "We were selling one-day-old raw whisky to the Americans," he boasted. "They paid us a dollar a gallon, when it might have cost them four times that. It was like selling futures." The operation was profitable from its first few months, but his partners sold out to a larger competitor, turning a handsome profit but losing their senior partner, who was enraged by their impatience. A similar experience followed in the late 1970s and early 1980s, when with a new set of partners Izzy bought out Monarch Life, the country's last major independent insurance company; when it became wildly profitable, the partners overruled him and once again sold out in 1983 to cash in on their investment. This time Izzy was so upset, he suffered his first serious heart attack.

Over the years, Izzy became disillusioned with law and business. In 1970, he decided to enter provincial politics, and almost overnight he found himself leader of Manitoba's

Manitoba Club
Winnipeg

minuscule Liberal Party. "If Louis Riel were alive today," he declared as an opening gambit, "I would be in the trenches with him." The Metis leader was put to death because he refused to hide behind an insanity plea that could have saved his life, so supporting him seemed to be the perfect qualification for the Liberal crown.

In the 1973 election, Izzy won his riding by only four votes, earning the title "Landslide Asper." The definite low point of the campaign occurred when New Democratic Party (NDP) premier Ed Schreyer referred to Asper, and Progressive Conservative (PC) leader Sidney Spivak, who was also Jewish, as "the gold dust twins from River Heights." (Labour minister Russ Paulley actually came up with the line, as noted by a *Winnipeg Tribune* story on June 20, 1973.)

The premier had likely not intended it as an anti-Semitic jibe, yet the portrayal of Spivak and Asper as rich lawyers left a bad taste in the mouths of Winnipeg Jews. Sidney Green,

running for the NDP (who, along with Saul Cherniack and Saul Miller, was a Jewish NDP cabinet minister), recalls it as "one of the less palatable features" of the contest, adding that Cherniack "pleaded with Schreyer to desist in adding fuel to this fire." Asper also received vile letters with a strong anti-Semitic undercurrent and decided to leave politics behind, though this decision owed more to the limitations of his position as provincial leader than to his being Jewish. Around the same time, in 1975, Sidney Spivak was replaced as PC leader when it was not-so-subtly insinuated by some party members that Manitoba would never elect a Jewish premier. But even after he left politics, Asper could not escape anti-Semitism. Any guy whose first name is "Israel" presents a natural target. Sometimes it was the silent treatment, such as not being hired as a tax advisor by the WASP-dominated grain trade. At other times, it was simply deliberate exclusion.

The mark of having "arrived" in Canada in the 1960s and 1970s was membership in one of the favoured dining clubs, where the chosen few smugly convinced themselves they belonged to a select assemblage of men who *are,* instead of men who merely *do.* These clubs were sacrosanct, set apart by the holy hush of privilege that endured undisturbed. Membership signified that the right connections had been made and the future was clear of ordinary concerns. All of these clubs were restricted to non-Jewish members. One of the last to demolish that restriction was the Manitoba Club. The first attempt to dismantle the non-Jewish barrier was sponsored in 1968 by James Richardson, dean of the grain trade, who invited Sol Kanee, an active director of the Bank of Canada, former chairman of the Royal Winnipeg Ballet, and all-round good fellow, for lunch. Richardson was severely reprimanded. The club did not admit its first Jewish member, Gerald Libling, until 1972. Israel Asper was refused membership to the Manitoba Club until the mid-1970s when, under pressure from the enlightened Winnipeg lawyer Alan Sweatman, the club finally passed a non-discrimination bylaw.

There followed other investments in Izzy's business life: an incarnation as a merchant banker and the acquisition of a television syndicate, which Asper built up to become Canwest Global Communications Corporation, Canada's largest and richest media empire, with significant international holdings. And yet his professional life never stopped being a struggle between the impossible and the desirable. His motto, reproduced on his family crest, was "Reach for the stars." And he always did.

ALTHOUGH IZZY ASPER gradually eased himself out of active corporate command of his media empire, he continued to bubble enthusiastically, "Even when I'm ninety I'll still be buying green bananas and looking for a thirty-year closed-end mortgage." In fact, he had officially turned over management of Canwest to his youngest son, Leonard, in 1999, naming him president and CEO, while he remained an active executive chairman. By 2003, he had stepped down from that office as well, prompting Leonard to muse at the Canwest Chairman's Dinner that winter: "What will this mean for me—Izzy stepping down as chairman? Nothing. I always get in the last words, 'Yes, Dad; No, Dad; *Right Away, Dad!*' "

As he passed the direction of the family empire to the new generation of Aspers—Leonard, Gail, and David—Izzy took a much keener interest in his "fourth child," the Asper Foundation, established in 1983. That was the year he gathered his children, then in their bursting twenties and not yet in the family business, for an important meeting. "We sat down in my boardroom at home," he recalled, "and I told them I had just incorporated a new company. I said that they should understand that they were all going to inherit equally, but there would be four children instead of three. So instead of

15

one-third each, it would be one-quarter. 'You've got a new sibling,' I said, 'and it's called the Asper Foundation. We just incorporated it. And I want you to be on side with this, because it will be the glue in your relationship. You can fight all you like about the business, but what will keep you together as a family will be the foundation. It will give you the opportunity to do something useful with your lives and make a difference.' "

Asper was generous to a fault, and that "fault"—if it was one—was that, unlike most other philanthropists, his original gift was only the first step in the process. Richard Leipsic, Canwest's senior in-house counsel who negotiated most of the donations, recalls that "people were always very surprised, because I was doing most of the legal aspect of the philanthropic deals, when I'd present them with a ten-page agreement ... Donating to the universities, for example, they got very befuddled about the fact that we were willing to give money, yet expected to have some commitment on the

other side, some accountability, some penalties if they didn't perform. Izzy always said that it was really easy making money; the hard part was giving it away. He realized that you don't get it back, that the return it shows is not monetary, it's in terms of its results, and I think he always had this concern that people would view it as their own money. If somebody comes in and writes you a cheque for $1 million, you don't necessarily feel the same accountability as if you had to earn it. So he tried to impose a measure of accountability on his charitable giving."

There was a tough, unsentimental side to Asper, expressed in his personal dictum: "You can't legislate propriety or morality or love or affection or loyalty. You can only legally cover what happens when they don't exist." Apart from his numerous and continuing donations to Israel, most of his charitable gifts were designed to improve Winnipeg's quality of life, focused on—but not limited to—its Jewish institutions. "Izzy infused the city with a tremendous vitality,

his *own* vitality," remarked Martin Freedman, a frequent law partner.

Between September 1999 and July 2000, Izzy Asper donated significant sums to his community and Israel. These included $10 million to the Winnipeg Foundation and the Jewish Foundation of Manitoba, $5 million to the Hebrew University of Jerusalem, $5 million to the St-Boniface Hospital Research Foundation, and $10 million to the University of Manitoba's business school, which was renamed the I.H. Asper School of Business in his honour. He felt he had paid back most of the dues he owed his community. "My job now is to do something that nobody else is doing," he told Moe Levy, the Asper Foundation's executive director and Izzy's chosen instrument to mastermind his grandest project. "I don't want this foundation just to be writing cheques. Let's do something that's fantastic and extraordinary for the world," Asper said. That fantastic venture turned out to be the Canadian Museum for Human Rights.

The senior Asper's obsession with human rights bloomed on October 14, 1970, when he arrived in the Manitoba legislature as leader of the provincial Grits. Asper, not quite forty years old at the time, was concerned about one issue only: the need for a provincial bill of rights. He promptly introduced his version, parts of which became the template for similar bills in other jurisdictions. In 1960, Asper had actively supported Conservative prime minister John Diefenbaker's pioneering Canadian Bill of Rights. In 1982, he was one of the leading provincial activists who championed Pierre Trudeau's Canadian Charter of Rights and Freedoms. "I went to Trudeau and put the proposition to him that this was such a monumental achievement, it ought to be celebrated in some tangible way just like the American Declaration of Independence," he recalled. "He loved the idea but his agenda was full and he just couldn't get at it." Izzy's own active political career cratered in the next election campaign

when he could not win more than the same five seats the Liberals had won in the election of 1969.

Decades later, beginning in 1997, Izzy, through the Asper Foundation, created an annual education and travel program for Canadian students to visit the United States Holocaust Memorial Museum in Washington, D.C., so they could bear witness to how a people can lose their rights, their freedoms, and their lives. It was a highly successful venture and helped reverse much existing indifference. But to create change and make a lasting impact, the number of people participating in this program needed to increase. Yet, the program was also

dealing with other issues: at that time, the Canadian dollar was at an all-time low against the U.S. dollar, so trip costs were becoming prohibitively expensive. Also, the program focused mostly on American notions of freedom. In spring of 2000, Gail Asper suggested to her father that ways to make this a Canadian journey needed to be explored. What was required, she said, was not only to teach Jewish children, and familiarize them with the horrors of the Holocaust, but to teach all Canadians about genocides and their warning signs, from a Canadian perspective.

On July 18, 2000, with martinis in hand, Izzy Asper and Moe Levy, whom Asper had hired

nine months earlier, discussed the concept of building a "museum of tolerance" in Winnipeg. It was a visionary project that would portray the agonies of human rights violations that blot history, and celebrate its heroes. The notion of exposing Canadians—especially during their youth—to the very worst abuses of human rights built upon the Washington experience, but the Canadian museum Izzy envisioned would create a national education program and bring in twenty thousand students from across Canada each year.

Little did Izzy realize that this vision would take more than a storm-tossed decade of wrangling to complete. The ostensible reason, as with most bureaucratic undertakings, was that nobody was willing take decisions that might set precedents. Not to worry. Not for a split second did a single individual involved with this mother of a project ever consider the idea that this would become a template. Not this side of sanity. It was strictly a one-off.

above Students explore the United States Holocaust Memorial Museum. The success of the Asper Foundation's Human Rights and Holocaust Studies Program trip to Washington inspired the decision to build the CMHR.

02

WINNIPEG: DREAMS AND REALITIES

IN THE PAST, Winnipeg's attractions—such as the Forks, Assiniboine Park, and the Exchange District—ranked among Canada's best-kept secrets, and loyal citizens preferred to keep it that way. Their love of Winnipeg was regularly tested in bitter contests with two of nature's most potent terminators: frost and floods. And yet, western Canadians retained an institutional memory of sorts.

Winnipeg's biggest problem was never the lack of a colourful history, but how much history it had to live down. It is the Vienna of Canada, an empire city without an empire—the Chicago of this country. What might have been, and should have been, was best summed up in a dispatch to the *Chicago Record Herald*'s correspondent by William E. Curtis, who visited the city in September 1911: "All roads lead to Winnipeg," he wrote. "It is the focal point of the three transcontinental railway lines of Canada, and nobody, neither manufacturer, capitalist, farmer, mechanic, lawyer, doctor, merchant,

priest, nor labourer, can pass from one part of Canada to another without going through Winnipeg. It is a gateway through which all the commerce of the East and the West, and the North and the South must flow. No city, in America at least, has such absolute and complete command over the wholesale trade of so vast an area. It is destined to become one of the greatest distributing commercial centers of the continent as well as a manufacturing community of great importance."

At the time, Winnipeg could (and did) boast of having more millionaires per acre than any other Canadian city. In its edition of January 29, 1910, the *Winnipeg Telegram* smugly reported there were nineteen millionaires in town but that the list "could be extended to twenty-five without stretching the truth," and then pointedly added: "The *Telegram*'s Toronto correspondent in writing a list of the millionaires of the Queen City, only put the list at twenty-one."

PORTAGE AVENUE WINNIPEG.

23

It was, above all, a grand time for the grain trade, especially for its leader, James Richardson & Sons, which delivered the first lake shipment to Port Arthur in 1883. The business spawned the Winnipeg Grain Exchange five years later, and it was there, amid the raucous bidding of its trading pit, that new fortunes were made. "In its heyday during the 1920s and 1930s, when the action in the trading pits was hectic, the Winnipeg Grain Exchange epitomized the capitalist spirit that had built the city," wrote the Exchange's historian. "This was free enterprise's finest hour as millions of bushels of wheat were traded daily. Then, exchange seats went for nearly $30,000. The Exchange put Winnipeg on the international map. As a leading North American commodity market, it linked the city with the other great world grain and financial centres of New York, Chicago and London."

The Richardson family that dominated the Exchange depended on their combination of Irish shrewdness and Loyalist sobriety to spin the dollars, enlarging their fortune and multiplying their influence through succeeding generations of astute dealing. In 1993, Hartley, who represented the family's eighth generation, was appointed president of the firm, and it was his family who later contributed $3 million to the Canadian Museum for Human Rights.

By 1911, Winnipeg had grown into the country's third-largest city, with twenty-four rail lines servicing its two hundred wholesale warehousing operations that sold goods across western Canada, and a growing population of 200,000. Banks and other financial institutions had elaborate regional headquarters here. These magnificent Edwardian structures—numbering well over a hundred, spread over twenty blocks

mostly on and off Main Street—combined Romanesque Revival architecture with exuberant overlapping mixtures of Tudor, Italian and French, or German Gothic. They were designed to impress borrowers and depositors alike, and it was from these money palaces that the original development of the Canadian West was financed.

The magnificent bank branches stand silent and empty now, their portals boarded up, monuments to Winnipeg's gilded age. "Winnipeg made the West," wrote Robert Collison about his hometown in a 1977 *Saturday Night* magazine article, "created it in its own image to serve its own needs and appease its own appetites. It carved a civilization, and an agrarian business empire, out of the unwelcoming prairie flatlands."

The Winnipeg grain merchants made inordinate profits, though they stoutly maintained that their commissions added only a quarter of a cent to the price of a bushel of grain. When a veteran Saskatchewan farmer came to town, James Richardson drove him around Wellington Crescent and the avenues that run off it, pointing out the grain dealers' impressive mansions. The puzzled visitor's only comment was "All this on a quarter of a cent?" There is no record of Richardson's reply.

The Canadian West is a land of long memories. During the Great Depression in the 1930s, Canada's plains suffered one of the worst drops in living standards anywhere in the civilized world. The money that wasn't lost during that fearful decade stayed frightened for a long time. A quarter of Winnipeg's houses were owned by the city for back taxes right up until 1941. That devastating interlude triggered the search for scapegoats.

The tendency to blame rich, eastern-based institutions and politicians for every disaster, whether it was drought or a plague of locusts, was rooted more in instinct than in considered thought, but it was no less powerful for all that.

Winnipeggers never felt sure whether they were in the centre of the country, or in the middle of nowhere. The roots of Prairie discontent stretch back to the turn of the nineteenth century when the western territories struck the bargains that brought them into Confederation. The prime issues were tariffs and freight rates, but more significant was the feeling that the industrialized East was using political means to subjugate the West and turn it into an exploitable backwater.

The original settlers had been at the forefront of Canadian civilization, with Winnipeg leading the way. They wrestled the country from wilderness, digging up and removing the stumps and rocks by hand and plow, turning forests and wild pastures into farms, villages, and towns. As the wartime and postwar industrialization of the Canadian economy took hold, they felt abandoned: their way of life lost, the existence they had invented out of hope and back-breaking labour given over to the navel-gazers and midnight philosophers from the big eastern cities, who had never served their harsh apprenticeships and didn't know the front end of a front-end loader.

Winnipeg always stood slightly apart from Prairie discontents and eastern metropolitan ambitions, historically acting more as an emporium than an independent power base. The great halfway house of the Canadian mosaic—the distribution hub for most of western Canada—Winnipeg lost that mandate in 1920 when the Panama Canal was completed and most of the traffic that had once moved overland through its gateways was permanently diverted.

In today's global economy, Winnipeg is doing its best with what geography has dealt it: a mid-continent location away from mountains and oceans. That translated into an ideal air traffic climate with no fog and user-friendly time zones. That in turn provided the city with an airport accessible twenty-four hours a day, 365 days a year, which its boosters intend to convert into a major international cargo hub. The deep-freeze winter chill remains a chronic condition, which may explain why some Winnipeggers pray for global warming. (That isn't true, but it sounds plausible.)

With some notable exceptions—none more assertive than the once rambunctious Asper clan—until recently there still existed a sense among the city's elite of being reduced to spectators in an increasingly metropolitan society. The sophistication was there, but Winnipeggers still lived on a human scale, one that allowed for the time to practise all the homely virtues. It was their pleasant habit to do a little business so they could socialize, instead of socializing to do business. That encouraged a mood of relaxed fatalism—a feeling that whatever happened here didn't really matter much, because no one stays mad or happy for very long.

It was into this context that Izzy Asper injected himself and his determination to upgrade his hometown. "I'm a pathological

25

Canadian and love Manitoba—I really do. I live
here by choice," Asper readily confessed. "I like
smaller centres, a simpler society, life is complicated enough. This is a kind of haven. Life here is
just what you see, there's no stratification; there's
no social classifications—just nice people. It's a
love of land, its strong pioneering roots of breaking that land and making a living out of it. And
because we're not large and because we're a long
distance from other major centres, there is a
tremendous esprit de corps in Winnipeg. Where
else would you get 50,000 volunteers out fighting
a flood?"

FOLLOWING HIS brainstorming session with
Moe Levy in the summer of 2000, Izzy was preoccupied with building a spectacular museum
and with the choice of its location. He went for
a midnight search across downtown Winnipeg.
Driving his black Mercedes, which was in reality an ultra-luxury sound system on wheels, he
found the ideal museum venue in the form of
an unoccupied gravel parking lot at the Forks. It
was an historic meeting place—its archaeological record reaching back six thousand years—at
the confluence of the Red and Assiniboine
Rivers. Although it was late, he immediately
telephoned Levy and excitedly conveyed his
orders: "I found it! I found the land . . . It's at the
Forks, and I want you to tie it up by the end of
the week."

A deceptively mild gent with a valiant
moustache, Moe had earned his spurs as Izzy's

confidant, trusted troubleshooter, and hit man.
The latter designation was based on the fact that
he was the only man west of the lakehead who
could out-stubborn Izzy. "Moe's personality was
very important," reflects Gail Asper. "He was
the opposite of Dad—low-key and without any
baggage. He was and is the master of diplomacy
and had the skill set to keep the project moving
forward."

Moses (Moe) Levy was born in Bombay
(present-day Mumbai), India, but his roots were
in Iraq. At the beginning of the twentieth century, his grandparents were among the many
Jews fleeing persecution in Iraq who wound
up in Bombay, where the prominent merchant
David Sassoon, also from Baghdad, had established a small yet vibrant Jewish community.
Levy's father supplied such products as chemi-
cals and dye to the Bombay textile industry.
However, within a year of India gaining its
independence in 1947, the extended Levy family
were making plans to relocate to the new state
of Israel and to London, England. Moe remained
in Bombay until 1968, then, at the age of nineteen, went to Winnipeg, where one of his sisters,
Malka, had already moved.

Everything in Moe's background made him
the perfect man for the job of working on the
museum. Levy received his bachelor of commerce (honours) and MBA in finance from the
University of Manitoba. He began his career in
government and achieved the position of man-
aging partner within the Manitoba Department

facing top Immigrants from Eastern Europe were not always welcome in Winnipeg when they arrived in the early years of the twentieth century, but they shaped the city's character in a lasting way.

facing bottom A street scene during the Winnipeg General Strike of 1919.

of Industry, Trade and Tourism. Between 1993 and 1999, Levy was the CEO and president of the Canadian Heritage Company, one of Canada's largest retail catalogue companies. He has also lectured on marketing, entrepreneurship, and small business at the I.H. Asper School of Business at the University of Manitoba. He and his wife, Barbara, have three children: Adam, Samuel, and Sarah. It is no exaggeration to say that, along with Gail Asper, Levy is primarily responsible for the CMHR becoming a reality.

Ever since that day in July 2000 when Izzy Asper and Levy toasted the concept of a human rights museum, most of the Asper Foundation's energies were concentrated on the creation of the Canadian Museum for Human Rights, with its focus on celebrating liberty and freedom of choice, and on transforming the prairie city of Winnipeg into a major tourist destination. The practicality of the project turned on government support at all three levels—municipal, provincial, and federal—which would break new ground not only in terms of the unusually high dollar amount required but also in its format, which would combine the public and private sectors in a highly original partnership. "We needed to have a sign from the federal government that it believed in Winnipeg, because Manitobans had lost hope and were leaving the province—they didn't think that anybody believed in them anymore," Gail Asper recalled. "There's a great saying from Samuel Johnson, 'Where there is no hope, there can be no

endeavour.' But you give people that one spark, and they are electrified. They can leap over tall buildings if they've got that hope. One of the reasons I fought so hard to keep this thing going is that people here do need hope. I look at the original bank offices built downtown at the turn of the century, and those magnificent, now abandoned but ornamental structures reflected people's self-image, and obviously they felt pretty darn good. But that was a hundred years ago. We haven't dreamed big for a very, very long time. And I learned something about architecture, which is put down these days as a big waste of money. But architecture is one of the most phenomenal ways to express your personal inner feelings about yourself. And it's permanent. How you present yourself to the world in a physical way, whether it's through clothing or architecture, sends important messages."

In many ways, Gail, born in 1960, had been preparing for this project her whole life. She followed in her father's footsteps and became a lawyer, obtained her bachelor of arts and LL.B. from the University of Manitoba in 1981 and 1984 respectively. After receiving her call to the bar of Nova Scotia in 1985, she practised corporate and commercial law in Halifax before joining the family firm Canwest Global Communications in 1989, as corporate secretary and legal counsel. She was a member of Canwest's board of directors from 1991 to 2010, and from 1998 to 2008 a member of the board of Great-West Lifeco and its subsidiaries. She serves and

29

has served on the boards of numerous not-for-profit groups, and co-chaired the $11-million endowment campaign for the Royal Manitoba Theatre Centre, which followed a $6-million capital campaign she co-chaired with Hartley Richardson. She then served on the board and as president of the Royal Manitoba Theatre Centre. She was the campaign chair for the Winnipeg 2002 United Way Campaign, and met every community leader during her tenure. She also served as past president of the board of directors for the United Way of Winnipeg. Fittingly, she has received numerous community service and humanitarian awards and was the 2005 recipient of the Ramon John Hnatyshyn Award for Voluntarism in the Performing Arts. Two years later, she was awarded the Order of Manitoba, and a year after that she was made an Officer of the Order of Canada.

Even with Gail taking charge of private fundraising, fuelled by an energy that could only be born of celestial sources, it is still difficult to believe that she plus Izzy and Moe were able to circumvent the three most formidable stumbling blocks in the project's realization: that it had to be built in the centre of Izzy's universe—in Winnipeg, Manitoba; that it had to win classification as the first national museum located outside Ottawa; and that it would be the only example of a major Canadian museum built with significant support of private enterprise. It was the trio's unlikely triumph in satisfying these tough-to-beat conditions that made the project possible.

facing A group of strikers overturn a streetcar during the Winnipeg General Strike of 1919. The strike pitted labour against business in a confrontation that tore the city apart for six weeks and impacted on local politics for the next four decades.

above The Winnipeg business district before the First World War.

03

A MAGNIFICENT CONCEPTION

IZZY ASPER WAS NOT a "journey is the destination" type of person. He was, affirms Gail Asper, a "just get to the destination" kind of guy. So if you had told him in early October 2003, prior to his death, that more than a decade later the Canadian Museum for Human Rights still would not be open, he would have been appalled.

Back in 2000, once the initial idea of the "Canadian Museum of Tolerance," as it was first referred to, began to germinate, and after Asper had found the spot at the Forks where he wanted to build it, plans advanced methodically and purposefully. Moe Levy soon would live and breathe the museum every day for the foreseeable future. His task was to study a number of history-oriented museums, including the Museum of Tolerance (MOT), which opened in Los Angeles in 1993 as a "human rights laboratory and educational center dedicated to challenging visitors to understand the Holocaust in both historic and contemporary contexts and confront all forms of prejudice and discrimination in our world today," as its website points out.

Although Asper had been sending grade nine students from across Canada to the United States Holocaust Memorial Museum (USHMM), he wanted a different kind of museum for Winnipeg—regardless of what his critics have suggested over the years. He was well aware of the major controversy that had erupted in 1996–97 over the proposed Holocaust gallery at the refurbished Canadian War Museum in Ottawa, and the decision to kill that gallery project after complaints by veterans, historians, and other interested parties. Asper's vision, perhaps not clearly articulated initially, was to establish a museum that would teach the lessons of the Holocaust as well as examine human rights in a Canadian context against the backdrop of the Charter of Rights and Freedoms. "He always knew," says Levy, "that there was a part of Canada's history that had never been told, and he spoke really with as much passion about the Holocaust as he did about the Japanese, Chinese, and the Aboriginal community in particular."

The project Asper originally envisioned was unique for several other reasons, factors that were to prove massive stumbling blocks difficult to hurdle. The grandeur of the museum Asper had in mind was akin to the Guggenheim Museum in Bilbao, Spain. But the Winnipeg museum came with a price tag in excess of $100 million—an amount that would double and then further increase, along with an estimated (and rising) $15 to $20 million in annual operating costs—and required an unprecedented public-private partnership. Such a project needed the full support and financial contribution of all three levels of government, with the bulk of the capital funds to come from the private donors and the operating costs to come from the federal government.

"One misconception that stands out is how people believed we intended this to be a private museum," Gail Asper recalled on the tenth anniversary of the project. "The opposite is true. Right from the beginning, my father stated that he only wanted to spearhead this project, not run it or control the agenda. That's what the Asper Foundation does: we initiate good ideas that may not come to pass if [others] don't get involved. But once they're on their feet, we move along. Our first letter and proposal to [the prime minister] Jean Chrétien in November 2001 proposes this as a national, federal museum."

A second, no less significant issue was that this was to be a partially funded national museum in Winnipeg, outside the National Capital Region—another first. In those early years, Asper somewhat underestimated the opposition he and his team were to face from just about every corner: skeptical politicians who questioned the need for such a mammoth and expensive museum; academics and journalists who did not believe a museum for human rights could be done properly or was even necessary; Ottawa bureaucrats and others who protested loudly about locating a national museum anywhere but in Ottawa; and a collection of naysayers and members of various ethnic organizations who questioned the Asper Foundation's use of taxpayers' money as part of an alleged scheme to advance so-called Jewish interests.

Yet, even if he had known of the multitude of obstacles that stood in the museum's path, Asper would never have quit. His political and business career had tested his mettle often, and always he had persevered. As Gail recalls about her father, "There's a great quote [that sums him up]—'Do or do not, there is no try. Let's just get the job done.' At the same time, he had a lot of times where he tried and tried and tried his best and he failed. But the bottom line is you keep trying, and persistence will pay off somewhere." Of any of Izzy's axioms to live by, that one proved to be the most relevant.

MEETINGS AND MORE meetings were the order of the day as Asper and Levy made the rounds. The purpose of their visits to provincial and municipal offices, even when the media

34

got wind of them, was deliberately kept confidential. From the start, Asper understood that the management of expectations around the museum had to be closely controlled. He rightly anticipated that as soon as news of the partially publicly funded project was known, hard questions would be asked, and he wanted to ensure that he had all of the answers to allay his numerous critics. First up were separate critical discussions with Winnipeg mayor Glen Murray and Manitoba premier Gary Doer.

Glen Murray and Izzy Asper had already clashed when the mayor had pushed through a ban on smoking in public places. "You can imagine," Murray remembered with a smile, "how well that went over with Izzy." Asper was renowned for his habit of smoking three packs a day. For this meeting, Murray agreed to give Izzy "a special dispensation" and permitted him to smoke in his office. With that issue settled, Asper enthusiastically launched into his pitch to Murray for a human rights museum at the Forks. Murray, who as the first openly gay mayor in

Canada had confronted his own share of human rights issues, was immediately impressed and promised his support. He pulled out a $5 bill from his pocket and signed it as the first down payment on the project. Within the next two years, that offer translated into a $20-million civic commitment, comprising approximately $11 million in realty tax relief, $6.7 million in land, and $2.3 million as a contribution to infrastructure (by 2012, the city's contribution eventually increased to $23.6 million).

Premier Gary Doer was next on the list. Like the mayor, Doer immediately embraced the museum. "Izzy has flair and a creative way of communicating, sometimes very graphically, his vision," says Doer, who has also served as Canada's ambassador to the United States. "But I remember it was two parts: [first,] it was going to be world class, and second, it was going to be a cultural institution outside Ottawa." Doer's only concern was about competition for federal dollars. Doer had been working with Ottawa and the government of Jean Chrétien

on a $700-million cost-shared flood protection megaproject, a consequence of the "Flood of the Century" that had crippled Manitoba in 1997. He feared (rightly, as it turned out) that Chrétien would play the two pricey projects against each other. Nevertheless, Doer committed the province to $20 million (an amount that would ultimately double) but made it contingent upon federal funding support.

Dealing with Prime Minister Jean Chrétien required more finesse. Asper's friendly relationship with Chrétien went back decades to when Asper was the leader of the Manitoba Liberal Party. Since then, he had supported Chrétien, and after Chrétien became Liberal leader in June 1990 and prime minister in November 1993, Asper had hosted Liberal fundraisers, making many personal donations to the party's coffers. At one of these political shindigs, they had a difference of opinion about the tax treatment of donations to private foundations, a debate Asper initially lost. Later, the tax change

Asper had argued for was implemented by the federal government.

Another consideration was that one of Chrétien's main goals as prime minister was to reduce the national debt he had inherited from Pierre Trudeau and Brian Mulroney. Hence, a request for a large commitment of federal dollars for a museum was naturally a touchy subject. "I am using my personal capital with the Prime Minister," Asper conceded in a note to Levy in mid-December 2000, "and I need to be able to show him that I'm not asking for anything unusual."

By the time Asper sat down with Chrétien at the Aspers' Palm Beach house in January 2001, Levy had fleshed out the museum proposal. It was a solid piece of work that delved into the history of human rights in Canada and gave Asper's vision a practical reality and early road map. Chrétien was impressed.

The document's mission statement said it all. The Museum of Tolerance, as it was still called, was "to defend, protect and encourage the pluralistic and democratic social order in Canada and internationally, by encouraging and promoting tolerance, understanding human and civil rights through information, education and research, facilitated through a unique public/private partnership; and to tell the story of the evolution of civil and human rights, and tolerance in Canada's own history, which is not unblemished, culminating in the patriation of the Constitution and the enshrining therein of the Canadian Charter of Rights."

The world-class museum was to be based in Winnipeg "as an international scale initiative that can educate Canadians, become a beacon of enlightenment for the world and make a difference in the fight against racism and intolerance." The proposed galleries were to include both permanent and temporary ones, as well as "a Tolerance Centre, an Avenue of the Nations, an international Learning Centre and a Human Rights Hall of Fame." Asper and Levy expected that the museum would be a national museum under the Museums Act, thus the federal government needed to take the lead regarding capital and operating costs. The board was to be appointed by the director of the museum, but with the approval of the federal cabinet. Although all of this seemed straightforward enough, what the precise role of the Asper Foundation would be was not spelled out—and indeed would become the nucleus of a tense and protracted lobbying effort and debate.

At the get-together in Florida, Chrétien liked the idea, especially its link with the Charter of Rights, which he had helped bring about as minister of justice in 1981. The prime minister told Asper that keeping the museum private made more sense, though he was prepared to match the private donations Asper raised. The next step was a feasibility study. Within a few months, largely through Chrétien's influence, the Asper Foundation received $700,000 for the study from the Western Economic Diversification Fund. The foundation kicked in an additional $100,000 toward the total cost of the $800,000 study.

Yet, there was already trouble on the horizon. In February 2001, Gary Doer accompanied Chrétien as part of a Team Canada visit to China. On the long return flight, Doer had an opportunity to chat with the prime minister about the museum and the Manitoba floodway project. As recounted by Dan Lett of the *Winnipeg Free Press,* Doer's recollection of the discussion on December 24, 2011, went as follows:

"Chrétien said to me [Doer], 'Choose one, because you can't have both the museum and the floodway.' It was my impression that he clearly wanted to do the museum. The floodway was just a big ditch. In terms of raw political sexiness, the museum was much better. He said, 'This guy Izzy, he really wants a museum. Let's do the museum for Izzy. We can do the museum now and leave the floodway until later. When you're in the central government, you have to balance your investments or you get into regional problems.' "

Doer said he thought the only way to get what he wanted was to pick the project Chrétien did not want to do: "I told him I wanted both, but that if we needed to do one first, he had to do the floodway. I told Chrétien that we'd both get crucified if we don't do the floodway first. I said, 'What are we going to do if we build the museum and then it ends up six feet under water?' " By the time they arrived back in Canada, nothing had been resolved and, adds Doer, Chrétien's position remained a firm "You have to choose."

In a similar vein, Gail Asper, after reading a letter in the *Winnipeg Free Press* about the need for government support of Aboriginal projects, including one at the Forks, cautioned her father about the intense competition for public money. "I think this is one area we need to really consider carefully in terms of ensuring there is unequivocal support for the project," she noted. "If at all possible, I would like to avoid an explosion of intolerance towards the Museum of Tolerance!" That insightful comment would prove to be more prophetic than she likely realized at the time.

By May, plans for the feasibility study were underway, as was the fundraising. Asper wanted the very best talent Levy could assemble to bring his vision of the museum to life. Levy started with Gail Dexter Lord of Lord Cultural Resources, based in Toronto, the world's largest cultural-planning firm. "Our

international reputation was important to Izzy," says Lord, "as well as our being Canadian." That first team included Lord and her team; Bill Barkley, a museum consultant from Victoria (who was later appointed to the CMHR's Board of Trustees); Robert Janes, a museum and heritage expert from Alberta; Bill Perlmutter of the Western Economic Diversification Fund office; Harvey Secter, then dean of the Faculty of Law at the University of Manitoba and an old friend of Izzy's; DeLloyd Guth, also from the Faculty of Law; and three prominent architects, two from Winnipeg, John Petersmeyer and Mike Scatliff, and one from Ottawa, Michael Lundholm. For months, they worked in secrecy using such code names as "Zebra" and "MOT," Scatliff remembers.

After much discussion, it was determined that the museum plan would focus on five major topics: the psychology of human rights, the Holocaust, Canadian stories, Aboriginal rights, and human rights actions and responses. Before the end of the summer, several other pieces had been put in place. The "Museum of Tolerance" had morphed into the more specific "Canadian Museum for Human Rights," and the fundraising organization, which was to be pivotal, the Friends of the Canadian Museum for Human Rights (or, simply, the Friends), was registered as a public charitable organization. The total price tag for the museum now was estimated to be $200 million, with operating costs of at least $16.5 million per year. Asper remained

confident that he could easily raise 30 per cent or $60 million of the capital cost.

The project also received the significant endorsement of Jim August, the CEO of the Forks North Portage Partnership, and of its chair, former Winnipeg mayor Bill Norrie, who oversaw the development at the Forks, where the CMHR was to be built. "We got a call from Izzy's office that he would like to meet with our board and outline his vision," August recalls. "Bill Norrie, at the time, had briefed me a little bit of what was going on here. So we got my board together and we went over and we sat in Izzy's boardroom. He sat at the head of the table and told his story, his vision of what he wanted to do, and that he wanted to do it at the Forks. It was amazing. You kind of get pulled in." The real challenge was negotiating a land lease deal. "We did actually go through a fairly protracted negotiating process," he adds, "but an acceptable arrangement on a ninety-nine-year renewable lease was eventually

agreed to." Later, when the museum became a federal institution, the land was transferred to the government.

Asper was always a tough taskmaster; he was famous for dictating sometimes scathing letters and e-mails, sent out by his secretary the next day with the notation "Dictated but not read." By the fall of 2001, Asper advised Moe Levy to accelerate the completion of the feasibility study, with Lord Cultural Resources continuing as objective consultants. Thereafter, Levy led the master planning, and communicated and advocated with the government and other funding partners. Lord Cultural Resources continued to be engaged in the project, and Gail Dexter Lord was the lead consultant at the April 17, 2003, announcement of the CMHR to the world. Her company provided the functional program that guided the architectural competition, as well as organizing, facilitating, and reporting on the cross-Canada consultations about the CMHR.

Some months earlier, on the advice of Lord, Levy also had his first meeting with Ralph Appelbaum, the talented head of the largest museum design company in the world, and most notably the chief designer of the USHMM. Appelbaum was soon selected as the chief designer of the CMHR's exhibits and content.

With key assistance from Lord Cultural Resources, Levy met the November 18 deadline that Izzy had arbitrarily given him. The exhaustive three-volume feasibility study Levy had written, and which had been scrutinized word for word by Asper, was ready to go. Levy made a strong case to locate the museum in Winnipeg, and estimated that it could draw 250,000 visitors annually. There was a proposed Tower of Hope as a defining symbol, and assurances that this was not to be an "Asper Holocaust Museum." Chrétien was captivated by the proposal. The capital costs had now increased to $200 million. According to Asper's blueprint, $100 million would come from the federal government and the balance of $100 million from the Province of Manitoba, the City of Winnipeg, and the private sector. In a letter to Chrétien on November 26, Asper guaranteed the private sector contribution of $35 million and asked the prime minister to set aside two hours for him by mid-December to review the package and establish a timetable for moving the project forward. It seemed that little could stop the museum's momentum now. Nevertheless, obtaining a firm federal commitment was to occupy a fair portion of Izzy Asper's time and energy for the next two years—tragically, these would be the last two years of his life.

MOE LEVY WOKE UP on Tuesday, April 2, 2002, to a headline story in the *Winnipeg Free Press* proclaiming that a $125-million Holocaust museum was to be built in the city, "a project being driven by the city's first family of media, the Aspers." Levy, in fact, had known about the pending story for a few days. He had been asked to comment about it, had politely refused, and had requested the newspaper not run the story because it was "too early to comment specifically on the museum project," but to no avail. Much of the detail, most importantly that it was a "Holocaust Museum," since the Asper Foundation was funding a program for Canadian students to visit the USHMM, was attributed to "unnamed sources" and nearly all of it was wrong. No matter; the damage was done and the unrelenting harsh criticism about to start.

Within a month, there was discussion that perhaps the Queen would participate in a groundbreaking ceremony during her upcoming visit to Winnipeg in October. The government's state ceremonial and protocol office was looking into the possibility. Asper, however, was growing increasingly frustrated, as he made clear in a letter to Doer on May 21, 2002. "One problem," he wrote, "is that while everyone endorses the project, none of the parties, other than us, has made either a percentage or a specific dollar financial commitment, each apparently waiting for the other. Something has to break the logjam, or we will be nowhere a year from now!" Asper's difficulty was that it was impossible to approach the private sector for large donations, since he could not yet confirm the government participation. On top of this, by July, the project's capital cost had risen to $224.5 million, and a month or so later it increased by another $45 million to $269.5 million, though that price tag now included new parking, the building of a dedicated youth hostel, and an endowment fund to support student travel.

Asper and Doer had another meeting in mid-July, and the premier agreed to recommend that the provincial cabinet approve 10 per cent of the capital costs ($27 million) provided that the museum design contained at least 60 per cent Manitoba content and the federal government committed to approximately $100 million. He also reiterated his position that flood protection and support for the museum should be considered separately, and not pitted against each other. A week after that, Asper met with Canadian Heritage Minister Sheila Copps and her deputy, Judith LaRocque. Copps and LaRocque seemed outwardly supportive, and Copps was enthusiastic about the Aboriginal content, which was to be an integral component of the museum. Asper and Levy attempted to propose then (and later) several federal funding formulas for capital and operating costs for a ten-year

period, but for the time being, the government remained quiet.

As the months passed, numerous back-and-forth discussions, primarily with Alex Himelfarb, the clerk of the Privy Council, on federal funding proceeded at a snail's pace. "We came very close to calling it quits a couple of times," says Levy. It also became clear that operating funds would never be forthcoming unless the museum became a federal institution, an eventuality that Asper did not oppose. But part of the holdup was the federal position that its contribution for the museum had to be from funds otherwise designated for federal projects (like the floodway) in Manitoba. Asper took great exception to this.

Near the middle of August, Asper encouraged Chrétien to act so that an official announcement could be made on September 11, 2002, symbolically on the first anniversary of the 9/11 terrorist attacks. There was no response from Ottawa, and Izzy's patience was wearing thin.

"You kept referring me to your Ministers and officials," Asper wrote somewhat more sharply to Chrétien on October 15, "but we have been offered every conceivable reason for delaying the announcement of Federal commitment until 'a more convenient time'... It's time to raise or lower the curtain. Jean, I simply can't wait any longer to announce the project...The dithering and delaying has caused many of the other players in this project to lose confidence in the believability of the Federal Government's 'commitment'... I appeal to you to join us now, and to end the bureaucratic nightmare." As for the allocation of the funds, he added, "With the greatest of respect, Jean, I vigorously disagree with this approach and, in fact, find it unsettlingly unfair. This is not a MANITOBA project—it is a CANADIAN project, located in Manitoba."

Needless to say, neither Chrétien nor Himelfarb were pleased with Izzy's blunt language. "I got a call from Alex," Levy recalls, "and was summoned to Ottawa for a meeting." Once there, Levy was kept waiting, and when he finally was able to speak with Himelfarb it was not, as he remembers, a pleasant encounter. "The conversation lasted all of a few minutes," Levy says. "Alex was angry and asked me, 'How could your boss dare to send such a letter to the prime minister of Canada? Go back and tell your boss that this project is dead.'"

Following the meeting, Levy, dejected, walked slowly down Wellington Street from the Langevin Block on Parliament Hill back to the Château Laurier hotel—a short journey that he and Gail Asper were to make numerous times over the next decade, usually after not receiving the answers they wanted about the government's support for the museum. That day in October 2002, Levy was despondent because he knew that if he told Asper what Himelfarb had said, the project truly would be dead before it was off the ground. Instead, he counselled Asper to take a step back and telephone the prime

minister to ease the tension. Asper agreed to do that, and the project indeed moved forward.

Finally, at the end of 2002, there was some good—though, from Asper's point of view, not great—news. Himelfarb, who had now calmed down, informed the foundation that the federal government was prepared to offer $30 million toward the museum's capital costs. More was promised toward Asper's objective of receiving a $100-million federal commitment. Yet this was critical: Chrétien might well have had in his mind that another $70 million would flow to the museum, but at no time did the prime minister or Himelfarb write anything down on paper about future funding support. Perhaps this tactic was taken to appease cultural administrators in Ottawa who disapproved of the project. Nevertheless, the absence of a paper trail was soon to have enormous ramifications.

Although Izzy Asper was not going to turn down $30 million, he was certainly not happy about it either and wanted to keep it quiet. "Dad was absolutely adamant he was not going to announce $30 million," Gail Asper later told the *Winnipeg Free Press* in a December 2011 interview. "It was not the $100 million we asked for, and at that point we didn't really know if we were going to get that." At yet another meeting with Doer, Asper presented the premier with a draft memo of understanding that stated that the province would commit $20 million regardless of what the federal government did. "Look, I'm not going to use this against you," Asper said to Doer. "I just need something to help me negotiate with the feds." But Doer refused to sign the document.

By the beginning of 2003, the project received the full support of Manitoba's five senators, Liberals and Conservatives. And Moe Levy and Gail Asper's appeal to Canadian ethnic and human rights associations also paid off when almost all of them publicly endorsed the CMHR. This included Aboriginal groups, such as the Assembly of First Nations and the Assembly of Manitoba Chiefs, though its leaders expressed concern about building a museum on potentially sacred land at the Forks.

An aggravating exception was an organization called Canadians for a Genocide Museum, which had ties to the Ukrainian Canadian Civil Liberties Association (UCCLA). The group complained that the proposed museum should not "elevate" one group's suffering above another's. In short, the group found it unacceptable that the CMHR would contain a permanent gallery with more floor space for (and thus giving more prominence to) the Holocaust than the Holodomor, the Stalin-inflicted famine in the Ukraine in the early 1930s that led to the death of millions of peasants. Asper wrote a strongly worded letter to Canadians for a Genocide Museum in which he attempted to allay the group's concerns. He also presented a strong argument that the Holocaust deserved a stand-alone spot in the museum because of the systematic nature in which one nation's resources, in this case

Germany's, were used to exterminate one particular ethnic and religious group. As additional events would show in the UCCLA's campaign against the CMHR, this historical question as to the unprecedented nature of the Holocaust was not easily resolved.

Levy had more success, at least initially, with the representative Ukrainian Canadian Congress (UCC), whose leaders were also suspicious that the CMHR was to be merely a "Jewish project," as Levy puts it. Asper was outspoken about his support for Israel and other Jewish issues, so the UCC's apprehensions were understandable. In early April 2003, UCC officials Paul Grod and Andrew Hladyshevsky accepted Levy's assurances that the Holodomor, as well as the internment of Ukrainians in Canada during the First World War, would be presented, as Levy explained in a letter he wrote on April 11, "very clearly, distinctly and permanently." He then added that "the intent of the museum is not to single out any one group but portray the human costs when human rights are abused"— words that were later to be disputed. As the museum project progressed, the UCC was to side with the UCCLA and argue that presenting the tragic story of the Holodomor in a gallery with other genocides, rather than by itself as was the Holocaust, was a slap in the face to an entire ethnic group.

By the spring of 2003, Levy and Gail Asper wanted to announce the federal funding of $30 million, but Izzy Asper was still reluctant

44

to do so. "I told Izzy that even though it's only $30 million, it's a start," says Levy. "We needed to show people, the donors, we were making progress. Let's do it one step at a time." Levy wore down Izzy's stubbornness, while Gail spoke to Sheila Copps. Everyone involved agreed to announce the CMHR at an event at the Forks on April 17, 2003, the twenty-first anniversary of the Charter of Rights. Copps agreed, and Izzy finally agreed to go along with the plan. "I had to convince him to do it," remembers Levy. "Alex Himelfarb had told me, 'Tell your boss to do it, [because] doing this one piece at a time is how this is going to happen.' Izzy wasn't buying it. Izzy wanted the whole $100 million and everything straightened out before he was going to come out and embarrass himself. He did not want anything half done."

At the event arranged by Levy, Asper was centre stage, along with Premier Gary Doer, Mayor Glen Murray, and, representing the federal government, Canadian Heritage Minister Sheila Copps. Conspicuously absent was Prime Minister Jean Chrétien, who was out of the country.

During the late morning of April 17, a crowd of six hundred invited dignitaries and guests gathered with great anticipation in one of the main buildings of the Forks market. The $30-million federal funding commitment was proudly announced by Copps, and Doer and Murray offered their commitments—although at this point, Doer was really only putting $6 million of a promised $30 million or so on the table.

Beyond the slick video presentations detailing the museum, the real star of the day was, of course, Izzy Asper, who received two standing ovations.

He declared that the CMHR would put Winnipeg on the world map. "Our development group," he said, "is totally convinced that the plan we have created will evoke an inspiring and sobering experience for the 300,000

visitors the museum should attract every year; that it has the potential to prove a beacon to the world; [and] that it will have a profound impact on and change the lives and outlooks of its visitors." More practically, he added that his goal was to have Ottawa dedicate 50 per cent of the total capital cost of the museum, estimated to be $200 million.

Mostly, though, he was relieved, as he made clear in his response to his friend, philanthropist Marjorie Blankstein, who sent him a note of congratulations a short time later: "Thank you so much for the good wishes and encouragement. I have been carrying this bag on my back for three years now, unable to talk seriously about it. Now, the wraps are off and I can go after it publicly. There are plenty out there who are trying to stop me. They are not people of good will ... Please wish me good health to have the fortitude to pull and push this thing through, so that when we are both old, [we] will attend the opening of this miracle."

THERE WAS A tremendous buzz in the city about the museum, which a *Winnipeg Free Press* editorial on April 19, 2003, rightly called "a magnificent conception." Plans were underway for an international architectural competition, and Izzy and Gail Asper and Moe Levy now turned their attention to raising $60 million—a task they were about to discover was easier said than done.

Gail was to be the anchor of the project, a job ten years later she has yet to relinquish. In a classic Izzy directive, Gail, as the head of the Asper Foundation, was instructed by her father that she was to now devote half her day, each day, exclusively to the museum.

"You must get up and end every day by asking, 'What did I achieve in finding $60 milion needed from the private sector for the museum?'" Izzy wrote in a dictated memo. "You are not to take any calls, answer any letters or have any meetings with people who are seeking donations from the Asper Foundation, as that is Moe's job and not to be duplicated … I am spelling [out] all of this, because this is your opportunity to prove that you can act like a senior executive, and not be distracted by everything that happens to go by. I hope you can exercise the focus and discipline outlined above. Believe me, this is the way I have operated all my life, and in my opinion, it is the only way you can accomplish things that everyone thinks can't be done."

Gail readily concurred, but admits she had no idea what she was getting herself into. "I willingly chose the path of the philanthropy," she says. "But who knew that it would mean seventeen thousand trips to Ottawa, criss-crossing the country grovelling for cash and never, never missing an opportunity to take a meeting with a government person. It's like when you're building a business, you don't have the luxury of saying, 'I can let this opportunity pass.' Until you get what you need, you don't know how much is enough. You'll never know that if you didn't do that meeting that might have been the pivotal meeting. I know I work hard, but when you're inexperienced, you don't know what you need to do to get something done. I didn't ever want to fail on the basis that we didn't work hard enough. I kept telling myself this in the darkest, darkest times, 'Okay, just calm down. Just remember that you can only do so much, and if you fail, you tried your best and that's all you can do.' It was the only way to stay sane. In my mind, real failure is when you don't even try."

The Asper plan was simple enough to start with. Izzy had no intention of approaching six hundred people to ask them for donations of $100,000 each. Instead, he, Gail, and Moe, along with assistance from Babs, David, and Leonard Asper, would seek out ten wealthy friends and business associates and request that they each contribute $6 million. And before you could chant "Abracadabra," the private donation portion of the museum would be a done deal. Given that the Asper Foundation and Canwest Global were each to contribute $6 million, only another eight donors needed to be found. On the Asper list were such individuals and organizations as the Winnipeg Foundation, Randy Moffat, Charles Loewen, David Graves, John and Bonnie Buhler, the Richardson family, Gerry Gray, Marty Weinberg, the Tallman family, Art DeFehr, and Gerry Schwartz, Izzy's friend and former business partner.

Winnipeg businessman David Graves, the CEO and chairman of the board of IMRIS, a high-tech medical company (and the creators of the VISIUS Surgical Theatre) was first to be approached. Izzy expected that it would take a bit of chit-chat to obtain the answer and money he wanted. He was soon to discover how wrong that assessment was and how much patience—which Izzy did not always have—was required.

Gail related the story of that cold call to the *Winnipeg Free Press* in December 2011: "[Graves] was just about to leave for this big trip sailing around the world. And all I can remember about the visit was Dad breaking every fundraising rule I knew of. Of course, he wanted to smoke in David's beautiful home and David said to him, 'Uh, we don't have any ashtrays.' Dad took a piece of tinfoil out of the cigarette package and said, 'It's okay, I'll just make my own.' I told him he couldn't smoke inside David's home, so we went out on the patio in the back and had our meeting."

Graves did not agree to Izzy's request that day for $6 million, and neither initially did anyone else who Asper approached. "Dad really believed that these people were going to listen to his pitch and give him $6 million," Gail says. "And when they didn't, it really upset him. I don't think he had any clue [how difficult raising funds would prove]." Moe Levy has the same recollection: "He was extremely disappointed because once he started to make the rounds, he found that his vision was not really the vision that others shared. Some saw the project as an 'Izzy Asper Holocaust Museum.' Some saw this as a monument to Izzy. So he had a tough time. And he became very disappointed."

A more positive experience, though one Izzy would not live to see come to fruition, was his meeting at his office in the summer of 2003 with John and Bonnie Buhler of the very successful Buhler Industries, a large manufacturer of agricultural and construction machinery. John Buhler, from a family of Mennonite pioneers, had been born in Morden, Manitoba, 125 kilometres southwest of Winnipeg, close

to the U.S. border. After spending about fifteen years selling cars in Morden, at the age of thirty-eight Buhler purchased his first farm equipment company, in 1969. A decade later he began acquiring other agricultural firms, until he established Buhler Industries in 1994. Within six years, Buhler, who had a lifelong fascination with tractors, purchased the last remaining tractor manufacturing facility in Canada and renamed it Buhler Versatile.

As a couple, John and Bonnie are friendly folk. Their first meeting with Izzy was supposed to be about thirty minutes; it lasted more than three hours. The three of them shared a fondness for rural Manitoba, since Asper had spent his early years in the town of Minnedosa, as well as for the significance of philanthropy. The conversation eventually got around to the museum. It started out, John Buhler recalls, with Izzy saying, " 'John, we want to raise $60 million. We want to have ten people, who will all have a seat on the board, $6 million each. These ten people will run the museum because they'll watch their money.' That was Izzy. We drove home that afternoon, and I said to Bonnie or Bonnie said to me, 'I think we should do this deal.' " However, they decided to wait a little while before contacting Asper to confirm their donation. When they eventually tried to do so, it was too late.

A short time after Izzy's death, the Buhlers visited Babs and Gail Asper and told them they would contribute $6 million to the CMHR; the

top Buhler Hall, a vast gathering space named in honour of John and Bonnie Buhler, will welcome visitors as they enter the museum.

above At the end of March 2004, John and Bonnie Buhler of Buhler Industries donated $6 million to the CMHR.

donation was not officially announced until the end of March 2004. It was, as Gail recalls, an emotional moment. "I remember bursting into tears," she says. "I think they were very taken aback, but it was just such an endorsement of this vision and an endorsement of me and Moe Levy, who had no track record like my father. He made conditions that we had to meet certain targets, but he was certainly there for us when it really, really counted. We could take that $6 million and the Buhler endorsement and sell it to others." Fittingly, Buhler Hall is a vast gathering space that will welcome visitors as they enter the museum.

The Winnipeg Foundation, Canada's oldest philanthropic foundation, established by William Alloway in 1921, also came through. In the late 1990s, the foundation had partnered with the Asper Foundation in sponsoring fifty non-Jewish Winnipeg grade nine students to participate in the Asper Foundation's Human Rights and Holocaust Studies Program, which

culminated with a trip to Washington, D.C., and a visit to the USHMM. Following a luncheon meeting with Gail and Izzy, Rick Frost, the Winnipeg Foundation's CEO, presented the proposal to his board. Given the size of the request, the foundation board naturally moved slowly. Several of its members sat through another presentation given by Izzy about the CMHR.

"It was actually kind of funny," remembers Frost. "We got into the meeting [at Canwest Global's boardroom] and, of course, Izzy was a jovial guy and greeting everyone. Finally, he got down to making his pitch. He had his big TV screen at the front of the boardroom and he tried to turn it on and it wouldn't work. He was pushing different buttons and some of the people around were getting a little exasperated. I'm looking at him getting a little exasperated [too]. Finally, he said something like, 'Doesn't anybody in this building know how to run a TV?' The ice broke, of course, and everybody burst out laughing. He eventually got the thing going.

It was a very good presentation, and we heard all the things about the museum." Up to that point, the largest donation the foundation had ever made was for $1 million. Yet, in the end, the Winnipeg Foundation agreed to fund the CMHR $6 million, contingent on the project proceeding as presented to it.

Needless to say, Gail was thrilled at the news. "As I understand it," she says, "it was their board member Sister Lesley Sacouman, who I had known from my days at United Way, who inspired the rest of the board to support this iconic architecture, to support not just drop-in centres but [also] education on human rights. She was the one saying that her [Aboriginal] students needed to see their stories told. They need to feel vindication. They need to feel pride and feel inspired to reach for the stars. She couldn't imagine a better message for her students at the drop-in centre in Rossbrook House than this Canadian Museum for Human Rights. She could have easily said, 'Folks, are we out of our minds? What are we building big fancy museums for when we need to feed the hungry?' But she got it. That was one of the greatest things. I think it was people like her who convinced the Winnipeg Foundation to make a $6-million gift."

BY THE FALL of 2003, however, another problem loomed. More than a year earlier, on August 21, 2002, Jean Chrétien, under pressure from his Liberal caucus—and a disgruntled Paul Martin, who had resigned (or was fired, depending on whose view you accept) as finance minister on June 2, 2002—announced that he was stepping down as Liberal Party leader and prime minister in February 2004. The media speculated that Chrétien was staying on for another eighteen months specifically to thwart Martin's leadership aspirations. As it played out, however, Chrétien decided to leave office as of December 12, 2003.

During this period of uncertainty in the summer and fall of 2003, Izzy Asper astutely reached out to Paul Martin, who he had also known for many years, and who Asper (and everyone else) knew would be the new Liberal leader and prime minister once Chrétien departed. Along with one letter written at the end of August, Asper sent Martin a package of information about the museum and urged him to "take time to refresh your memory about this project so that we can have a meaningful discussion." Asper added that he was hoping to

meet with Chrétien soon "to see if we can convince him to publicly declare the remaining $70 million so that it can be booked in the current fiscal year."

Izzy and Gail also had a productive meeting with Manitoba Liberal MP Reg Alcock, who was expected to be appointed to a position in the Martin-led cabinet. "We knew we were speaking to someone who really 'gets' what we're trying to do with the Museum, not just from an economic standpoint, but from the historical and spiritual standpoint as well," Gail wrote to Alcock in early September. And, she added for good measure, "we really appreciate your assistance in confirming the balance of the capital funding from the federal government as well as the promised operating funds." There would be more talk of that in the near future.

Certain that he could convince Chrétien to confirm the federal donation before the prime minister retired, Izzy took advantage of the opportunity presented by Chrétien's visit to Winnipeg for a Liberal Party fundraiser and farewell dinner at the Fairmont Winnipeg hotel. On Friday evening, October 3, 2003, Asper and Chrétien were able to speak privately for a few minutes. Following that discussion, Asper was elated and told Moe Levy that Chrétien was prepared to announce another $40 million immediately, with the balance of $30 million to be made before the end of the year, contingent on confirmation of like amounts from private donors. "Moe, we got a deal," he said to Levy.

"They're going to give us an additional $70 million. It's in the bag as long as we can prove we can raise our money."

Monday evening, October 6, was Yom Kippur, the Day of Atonement. Izzy was feeling good as the Asper family gathered at Gail's house that night for the traditional break-the-fast dinner. Daniel Asper, David's thirteen-year-old son, remembers that his grandfather was sitting in the living room having a glass of red wine and a cigarette. "I waved goodbye to him," says Daniel, "and he winked at me and waved back."

Izzy and Babs had recently sold their house near the corner of Wellington Crescent and Ash Street and moved to a newly constructed, elegant double-storey penthouse condo at the foot of the always fashionable crescent. There were boxes still yet to be unpacked, and the movers and interior designer had arrived early the next morning, Tuesday, October 7. While Babs coordinated the action on the main floor, Izzy was preparing to travel to Vancouver with Gail and Moe. On the initiative of Phil Fontaine, the national chief of the Assembly of First Nations, Izzy was invited to attend a special meeting of the assembly to announce the international architectural competition, as well as to deliver a speech about how Aboriginal history would be an integral component of the museum. He was to be given a mask as a gift and bestowed with an Aboriginal name.

"Some problem arose," Babs later recalled, "and I called to him to ask where to put some-thing I called and called, and it didn't surprise me that he didn't hear. So I went upstairs and found him lying in the closet." She tried to help him, then called an ambulance, but it was too late. Israel Harold Asper, entrepreneur, lawyer, media tycoon, philanthropist, politician, jazz aficionado, and human rights advocate, was dead at the age of seventy-one.

Sad proof of Izzy's impact on Winnipeg was most visible at his funeral two days later, at the Shaarey Zedek Synagogue. It was nothing like the city had ever seen. Nearly two thousand people filled the synagogue to pay their last respects to Asper. Everybody was there, including four sitting or former prime ministers—Jean Chrétien, John Turner, Paul Martin, and Stephen Harper—none of whom were speaking to one another. One of the memorable sights of that day was watching the private jets, stacked three high, waiting to land at the airport and disgorge their distinguished personages. More important, the city turned the burial into a state occasion.

Rabbi Alan Green, who presided over the service, rightly put the sombre occasion into perspective:

Israel Harold Asper was a human being like the rest of us. He had the same seven days a week, and twenty-four hours a day as the rest of us. He had two hands, two feet, and a heart and a brain, like the rest of us. But there was one critical difference

between Izzy Asper and ordinary men and women ... Izzy was one in a billion, a charismatic, creative genius who revealed the extent to which one person can positively impact an entire generation—not to mention generations yet unborn. Izzy wasn't a shul yid. But he was a genuine Jewish hero. In both their size and their number, Izzy's philanthropic projects were on a truly heroic scale. And his passionate, articulate defence of Israel and the Jewish people was a lone voice crying out in the wilderness. His chutzpah in confronting the anti-Israel bias of the international media was a constant inspiration to all who know how often reality runs counter to what we see and hear on the evening news.

So many mourners slow-marched their way out of the crowded synagogue, the funeral took on the air of a czarist cortège in a late-nineteenth-century provincial Russian town.

Helicopters hovered overhead as friends and strangers alike stood on the lawn listening to the eulogies delivered by the rabbi and Asper's children and friends. Of the many words spoken, none were as poignant as those of young Daniel Asper, who said the reason his grandfather's heart stopped "is because he put so much of it into the lives of others." As the hearse and cavalcade of black cars left Shaarey Zedek and headed toward Portage Avenue and then north down Main Street to the synagogue's cemetery, Winnipeggers lined the streets just to get a glimpse of Asper's final ride.

"People stood in front of their shops that were shut," recalled Jodi Lofchy, Izzy's niece. "Flowers had been put out on the street, and the people there saluted, or put their clenched fists over their hearts. It was magical." Diane Francis, the ace financial journalist, saluted Asper as "Canada's last Renaissance man." It is difficult, if not impossible, to imagine another Winnipeg Jew receiving such a royal send-off.

The last interview Izzy Asper had given was to Evan Solomon of CBC Television a few months before his death. Later, Solomon, who had never met Asper before, was asked what Izzy was like as a person. "To some people, Israel Asper was an adversary," he said, "but he was the best kind of adversary to have—the kind of adversary who makes you better at what you do, makes you challenge your own assumptions. They don't make people like that anymore. For his fearlessness, for his boldness, and his vision, Izzy will be missed all over the country."

Despite their enormous grief at his loss, Babs Asper and her three children—Gail, David, and Leonard—along with Moe Levy and lawyer Richard Leipsic, vowed the day of his funeral that the museum project would be completed. Premier Gary Doer was of the same mind. "There certainly was the resolve that we wouldn't let his legacy languish and fail and lapse because of his death," he says. "In fact, we had a moral obligation as well as a community obligation to get it done." Doer spoke to both Martin and Harper outside the synagogue, and both were in agreement with that sentiment. The next day Moe Levy received his first call from Arni Thorsteinson, a top-notch fundraiser and friend of Izzy's (who would later become the first chair of the CMHR), confirming his support and help to raise funds for the project and assist with government funding. Yet, future events in Ottawa were about to impose tremendous obstacles in the path of the Canadian Museum for Human Rights, political hurdles not easily vanquished.

04

FROM DESPAIR TO LIMBO

IT WAS AKIN to the unlucky Apollo 13 crew's cry from space, "Houston, we've had a problem," or to what Gail Asper has called "the perfect storm." Izzy Asper was gone, and Jean Chrétien replaced as prime minister by his archrival, Paul Martin. The bitter feud between their fanatic Liberal loyalists had rocked Ottawa for several years. In his memoirs, Chrétien, who derisively refers to the Martinites as "self-serving goons," writes that he should have fired Martin as finance minister as early as 2000 but opted not to. Hence, Martin didn't leave the cabinet until mid-2002, then succeeded in forcing Chrétien to leave office a few months early, in December 2003. Martin won the Liberal leadership on November 14, 2003, and became prime minister on the day Chrétien resigned, a month later.

This double whammy for the museum was terrible. "Everyone thought the project was going to die," concedes Moe Levy. The Aspers had lost their husband, father, mentor, and leader, as well as what Gail deems their "political capital." Izzy opened doors in Ottawa and elsewhere that remained shut to mere mortals. Worse, the deal for the balance of the $100 million Chrétien had promised Izzy was agreed to on a handshake.

Paul Martin had known Izzy Asper almost as long as Jean Chrétien had. He liked and respected him—"I was a huge fan of Izzy Asper," he says—and indeed thought highly of the CMHR project even before he became prime minister. But there were several problems that nearly did kill the museum. For Gail Asper, her family, and Moe Levy, the two years of Paul Martin's prime ministership were the most difficult any of them had experienced.

The first big headache was the lack of documentation. "When I became prime minister," Martin explains, "I was unsure of the nature of the discussion that had taken place between the former prime minister, Chrétien, and Izzy." And, he adds, "of course, government operates on a slightly different basis than two friends shaking hands." That was the nub of it.

Next was the stiff, even intractable, opposition from within his PMO, cabinet, and the bureaucracy to funding a public-private national museum outside Ottawa. Toronto, perhaps, went the argument, but Winnipeg? That just seemed too provincial an idea for Ottawa mandarins, some Toronto Liberals, and most members of the Toronto-based media to wrap their heads around.

Martin, too, had his doubts. "My own view was, to begin with, that it's very important that Canada had a national capital where the majority of the national institutions are, and that it be a national capital which reflects the country as a whole," he explains. "That being said, we're a lot of geography in this country, and we're very few people. I did believe that national institutions should as well be outside the national capital commission." That included, he says, a human rights museum in Winnipeg. However, he also points out that this was not the majority view in Ottawa.

Gary Doer refers to this difference of opinion as a "clash of visions." "The cultural community in Ottawa," he says, "viewed all cultural institutions [as] having to reside in Ottawa. The vision of Izzy Asper and obviously all of us who supported the project, which built into a larger group than just Manitobans, was that a country like Canada could have a lot of [its] cultural institutions in Ottawa but also could have national cultural institutions outside Ottawa. So it was a clash of visions, but there was nothing personal about it."

Faced with a mounting national debt and confronted with the sponsorship scandal over allegations that millions of dollars had been doled out in Quebec by agencies with links to the Liberals, Martin and his team adopted a bunker mentality. Open infighting with the Chrétienites intensified, and Martin did not hesitate to cancel expensive Chrétien projects such as a proposed $90-million Canadian history centre and museum. Essentially, it was a given that if Chrétien was for it, Martin was most likely against it. And the Canadian Museum for Human Rights was caught in the middle of this feud.

Like her father, Gail Asper has never shirked from a challenge her entire life and was not about to now. Indeed, she faced it, as she usually does, with a smile. One former Canwest Global executive aptly described her as "being as effervescent as champagne." Added journalist Aliza Davidovit in a February 2012 cover story for *Lifestyles Magazine International,* "Gail is bubbly, delightful to the senses and leaves you wanting more. Her enthusiastic personality is infectious and once you've met Gail Asper, you just can't quite get her out of your system."

She has devoted the past decade to the CMHR, an experience that has more than lived up to another of her favourite quotes, this one from Calvin Coolidge, who served as U.S. president from 1923 to 1929. "Nothing in the world can take the place of persistence," Coolidge stated during a speech he delivered in 1933. "Talent will not; nothing is more common than unsuccessful men with talent. Genius will not; unrewarded genius is almost a proverb. Education will not; the world is full of educated derelicts. Persistence and determination alone are omnipotent." That was truly the story of the museum saga from 2003 onward.

MOE LEVY WAS just as determined as Gail to carry on. Two weeks after Izzy Asper's death, he arranged for the announcement of the

architectural competition, together with the official groundbreaking ceremony, to take place in Winnipeg on October 24. "Moe was able to just turn everything around," remembers Gail. "But it is October, so you have to remember that to have something at the Forks was not easy. It could be snowing or raining, so you have to have tents, and then you have to ensure all the protocols are followed. It becomes a pretty complicated event to pull together quickly. Moe, also reeling from the impact of Izzy's death, somehow just lined up all the people and the media. There weren't fourteen people to delegate the job to. It was Moe Levy who does everything from emptying the garbage to ordering the stationery to negotiating with the prime minister. Our family was still in a state of shock. We just stumbled out to this setting and found that everything was perfectly put together. We had all the dignitaries there, the media, and the special guests. To me that was the real achievement—that, through our grief, Moe pulled together a phenomenal moment."

Levy felt guilty for pushing the family to do it. "I felt it was important to assure the family and their supporters that we were going to fulfill Izzy's last wish," he says. "If we had waited a month, we could have had a major snowfall, and the archaeology work required would have been delayed about seven months until the frost had left the ground. A delay of that length could have spelled the end of the project." Instead, an iconic photograph of Babs and Gail Asper, both with shovels in hand, digging the sod,

57

announced that Izzy's dream of the CMHR was not done—not by a long shot. "We really wanted to show the world," Levy adds, "that this project was so important to the family and despite everything we were going ahead." It was as if the spirit of Izzy, with his legendary impatience, had been transferred to Moe. One of Izzy's mottos was "Delay is risk," and Moe was not going to take any more risks than were necessary.

As with each step in the museum's evolution, however, there was criticism. Although Phil Fontaine, the national chief of the Assembly of First Nations, was a museum supporter, he also expressed concern about public funding for the museum when funding for the Spirit Lake Aboriginal project at the Forks, a proposed First Nations cultural and spiritual centre, remained undeveloped and underfunded. There were questions, too, about the Winnipeg Foundation's $6-million donation when so much poverty existed in the city and elsewhere. And the Ukrainian Canadian Civil Liberties Association started a cross-Canada letter-to-the-editor campaign questioning the CMHR's purpose and plan, and disputing the historical argument that the Holocaust was "unique," as Levy had suggested in one press interview in late November 2003.

A month later, Gail Asper and Levy wrote a response addressing some of these critical comments in a letter published in the *Winnipeg Free Press:*

Concerns have been voiced with regard to the wisdom of The Winnipeg Foundation

making a significant donation of $6 million to the project when issues of child poverty, especially Aboriginal child poverty, still exist. We recognize the importance of doing all we can to address such issues. In order to alleviate poverty, education is essential. The CMHR will, for the first time in Canada[,] profile, among other things, the story of Canada's First Nations. This will be done not only in the Museum but in a course, which will be designed and taught in high schools across the country ... The message of the CMHR will be that of personal responsibility for the protection and advancement of human rights. We hope to instill a sense of leadership and empowerment to all who visit ... As far as the content of the Museum is concerned, we intend for the CMHR to tell the major Canadian human rights stories with key international stories also being highlighted to underline the message of the Museum— that of personal responsibility for the protection of human rights. There will be no "hierarchy of suffering," but we do intend to showcase in powerful and moving ways the human rights failings and successes in Canada primarily and in the world.

That noble objective was put to the test almost from the day Paul Martin became prime minister. It was as if Gail and Moe had to start their lobbying from scratch. Inside the Martin cabinet, their most reliable ally was Reg Alcock,

the MP for Winnipeg South who was made president of the Treasury Board, the minister responsible for the Canadian Wheat Board, and the minister responsible for Manitoba. Built like an offensive lineman, Alcock, who died suddenly in October 2011 at the age of sixty-three, was also as gentle and cuddly as a pussy cat. He had bought into the idea of the museum from the moment he had been briefed about it by Izzy and Gail, but he clearly had his work cut out for him in trying to convince Martin and his cabinet colleagues to fork over the balance of the $70 million promised by Chrétien. More than once, Alcock was forced to state publicly that he had no knowledge of what had transpired between Chrétien and Izzy,

and what precisely had been agreed to. As for the federal government coming up with the $15- to $20-million request for the museum's operating funds, that was an even more insurmountable problem, for which there appeared to be no satisfactory solution.

Throughout late 2003 and well into 2004, the correspondence and meetings between Gail, Moe, and Alcock—with input from Senator Richard Kroft, Liberal MP Anita Neville, and every other Manitoba politician in Ottawa—were constant. But Asper and Levy were up against a brick wall. Nothing changed no matter how frequently Gail wrote to Alcock or Martin explaining that time was of the essence and that it was impossible for her and her organization to successfully raise the required private funding without a public statement of the federal government's commitment.

"We simply can't remain in limbo much longer," she e-mailed Alcock in the middle of February 2004, urging him to arrange a meeting for her with Martin. "We need to know if we have a partner with the federal government at the $100 million level or not. If we don't, we need to know that, so that we can determine if the project can proceed." In closing, Gail quoted her father's remarks to the CBC's Evan Solomon in the last television interview he gave before he died: either the museum was going to be "an architectural icon and one that changed the face of Winnipeg and Canada," or it was not worth doing at all.

Alcock's progress was slow, even by Ottawa standards. Martin was knee-deep in dealing with the sponsorship scandal, and on February 19, 2004, he appointed Quebec jurist John Gomery to investigate it. The museum was hardly the first, or even tenth, thing on Martin's mind. When it did come up for discussion, Martin had determined that in line with the usual 50-50 federal-provincial cost-shared programs, if the federal government was to fund the museum with $100 million, the Province of Manitoba had to offer more than the approximate $30 million it was prepared to spend on the project.

In early April, Martin was flying to Winnipeg as part of his cross-country pre-election tour when he decided, on the spur of the moment,

that he would speak to Gail. Reg Alcock recalled his tense conversation with the prime minister as follows:

"We were flying in on the Challenger. He's coming to Winnipeg, I forget what for, and he tells me as we're coming in, [in] the last hour of the flight.

"He said, 'By the way, when we get to town, I'm going to see the Aspers.'

"I said, 'Good, well, I can see them.'

" 'No,' he said, 'you can't come. I'm tired of this, and I'm going to tell them $30 million and that's it. Take it or leave it. I'm sick and tired of this.'

"He really gave me a what for."

It didn't help that Martin had a bad cold. In Winnipeg, Anita Neville was notified by Martin's assistant to help arrange a meeting. "We pulled out all the stops to try to fit it in, since his time was very tightly scheduled," she says. "Ultimately, we got a meeting with him at the private Winnipeg airport used by private airplanes." By the time Neville arrived, Gail and Moe were already there, and Gail was brewing Martin a pot of herbal tea. The meeting was a disaster.

"We got fifteen minutes," Gail says. "He was sick as a dog. He had a cold. I remember bringing some special tea and making him [some] to try to soothe his raging throat. He just looked so tired and so beat. Then our DVD machine didn't work. We had a little DVD that really was fantastic, and we went to turn [on the machine] and it didn't work. We could not get it to work. I said, 'God is not being fair here.' We sent him the

DVD, but I doubt he ever watched it. So we made the pitch very quickly, but he was probably not paying attention." Martin departed Winnipeg without agreeing to anything, and it was left to Alcock to calm everyone down. "Just cool your jets," he told Gail and Moe. "Don't react. Leave it with me and I'll see if we can work it out." More than once, Gail and the Asper family contemplated packing in the project.

Less than two months later, Martin requested that the governor general, Adrienne Clarkson, call a federal election, to be held on June 28. His intention was to clear the air of the ramifications of the sponsorship scandal and rid his government of the last vestiges of the Chrétien legacy. The election results, instead, showed the public's anger over the daily revelations of the scandal at the Gomery hearings and a significant decline of support for the Liberals (especially in Quebec)—a downward trend that eventually bottomed out seven years later with the shellacking the party took in the election of 2011. On June 28, 2004, however, Martin, who had earned the unflattering nickname "Mr. Dithers" for having taken so long to call an election, now had to accept that he ruled over a minority government. The reborn Conservative Party led by Stephen Harper had done better than expected, despite stumbling out of the gate and not always keeping the more extremist members of its caucus in check.

This new dynamic in Ottawa meant that Martin and his government were distracted by

a long list of other issues besides the museum. Yet, there was another factor that kept coming up in Gail Asper's ongoing discussions about the project. Lurking in the background of the decision on the museum was the unhappiness of Martin and his advisors with what they perceived to be the negative tone toward the government published almost daily in the *National Post,* then owned by the Aspers' Canwest Global Communications. True, the *Post,* as well as other Canwest newspapers such as the *Ottawa Citizen,* was tough on Martin and the Liberals. Indeed, the *Post* had endorsed Harper and the Conservatives five days before the vote with the stinging rebuke that "the Paul Martin" who slew the deficit as finance minister "does not seem to be the same Paul Martin campaigning for a mandate as prime minister." Still, with the exception of the *Toronto Star,* generally a reliable fan of the Liberals (though even its assessment of the Liberals was not entirely positive in the spring of 2004), Canadian newspapers for the most part, including the *Globe and Mail,* were equally critical of Martin and his team. Nonetheless, the perception of this connection between the museum and the *Post*'s coverage remained prevalent in government circles.

"Certainly some of the guys on his staff hated the *National Post,*" admitted Reg Alcock. "Paul would get angry at articles... It's not like the *National Post* was absolutely fixated on screwing Paul Martin. So at that level, I've never heard Paul personalize it. I think there were concerns about David [Asper, the chairman of the *National Post*], seeing him as sort of a political activist. In my world, that wasn't as big an issue. But certainly to some of Paul's staff, it was—no question. And he was close to his staff."

Anita Neville concurs with that analysis. "One of the overriding factors probably in the larger caucus and certainly among the leadership was the hammering that the *National Post* was doing to us. Oh yes, it was a significant piece of it. I mean, they were just going after us full force, and I know that I made the argument many times to separate out the newspaper from the museum … But there was a view out there about how do we support somebody who is trying to take us out? That was prevalent; it was spoken of many times, not only by elected officials but by [individuals] around the prime minister."

This was exactly the same message Gail was receiving. In early August 2004, she had a pointed conversation with Ed Lumley, a former Liberal cabinet minister and a close friend and advisor of Martin's. "He reiterated that there is absolutely nobody in the PMO that will recommend this project right now because of the 'relentlessly vitriolic treatment' the Liberals received from the [*Ottawa*] *Citizen* and the *Post*," she reported to her family and Moe Levy. "Ed chastised me and said that during the election campaign the *Post* was utterly without balance and that there's no way Dad would ever have allowed the *Post* to endorse anybody but his respected friend Paul Martin." Her advice was

to address the issue matter-of-factly: in the future, the Canwest newspapers would strive to have more balance.

Nothing had changed, however, six weeks later. In a discussion with John Harvard, a former Manitoba MP who had been recently appointed the province's lieutenant-governor, Gail's worst fears were confirmed. "The stalling in the Government funding is still directly the result of the *Post*'s treatment of the Liberals and its constant Liberal bashing," she reported. "The feeling is that they're going to let us squirm and be punished and that there is the feeling both among Winnipeg Liberals and Ottawa Liberals that we have a lot of gall in expecting any favours when we first trounced the Liberals for too much spending and then expect them to come up with $100 million."

Such an accusation angered David Asper, who argued that the *Post* issue was being used merely as a convenient excuse not to fund the museum. "The *National Post* editorial position regarding fiscal policy has been consistent from the day it started and was not invented when Paul Martin took office," he wrote a week later in reply. "Indeed when Martin took office we encouraged him and applauded his election as leader of the party … Moreover, to suggest that we 'first trounced the Liberals for too much spending' totally belies the facts and I urge you, for the sake of clarity, to look at the Liberals' own house organ, the *Toronto Star,* to see the treatment the Liberals got in that newspaper as well as in the *Globe and Mail*."

THE RECRIMINATIONS about the *Post* all took place behind closed doors. Meanwhile, in the months after the election, a public debate ensued about what specifically Jean Chrétien had guaranteed Izzy Asper. "Ottawa says it never promised Winnipeg human rights museum $100 million," a *Canadian Press* wire story declared on July 7. Curiously, the story had originated from Reg Alcock's office. "There was a handshake. Nothing was signed," claimed Lise Jolicoeur, Alcock's spokesperson at the Treasury Board. Two days later, Alcock, speaking on the radio with Charles Adler, stirred the pot again. For the first time, Alcock stated publicly that he was uncertain whether he could deliver the balance of $70 million. The Aspers "created a business plan that [the federal government is] to pay 50 per cent," he told Adler. "There's no record that we've ever agreed to that."

The next day, July 8, former federal cabinet minister Sheila Copps, a Chrétien loyalist who had been defeated on June 28, stated in an interview with the *Winnipeg Free Press* that "the government had agreed to contribute $100 million toward the building of the Canadian Museum for Human Rights in Winnipeg, provided the private sector raised the same amount." By this time, Gail had spoken to Chrétien, who did not wish to issue a public statement himself lest it be perceived by Martin and his PMO as meddling, and she told the *Winnipeg Free Press* that the former prime minister "confirmed what we've been saying all along. An understanding absolutely existed," then adding, "At least

it shows we're not crazy." These statements of support were called into question when another Chrétien loyalist, Senator Sharon Carstairs, told the *Free Press* that "there was never a clear commitment about a 50-50 cost sharing of the project" and that she "was never told there was a hard and fast agreement in place to provide the whole $100 million."

Like rubbing salt in an open wound, further commentaries about the confusion and the museum quickly appeared in Toronto newspapers, several of which had already made it clear that they thought the museum was a bad idea. "While one can sympathize with the Aspers' concerns [about the $100-million funding]," Peter Worthington wrote in his *Toronto Sun* column on July 13, "it also seems hard to justify the government contributing such a huge amount to a human rights museum, regardless of how worthy such institutions are."

Raymond Heard, a communications consultant and lobbyist, and a former Global television executive, who was providing Gail, Moe, and their team with media advice, sprang into action. From his office in Toronto, where he was keeping track of the negative commentaries, Heard urged Gail and Moe to stress the number of jobs the museum would create and to seek out a wide range of influential individuals, such as former New Brunswick premier Frank McKenna, who served as interim chairman of the Canwest Global board following Izzy's death (and whom Martin would appoint as Canadian ambassador to the United States in March

64

2005); former prime minister John Turner; Liberal senator Jerry Grafstein; and Gerald Schwartz of Toronto-based Onex Corporation and Izzy's one-time business partner, who was close to Martin, to speak out in favour of the project. Within a week, Heard reported that he had had a difficult time convincing several key cabinet ministers and backroom advisors that the Aspers (and their newspapers) were not hostile toward the Liberals.

Moe Levy, who had little patience for this petty excuse of blaming negative Canwest newspaper coverage, was understandably exasperated by the government's position. "It's been a very patient 15 months trying to get an answer," he wrote to the Asper Foundation trustees. "We have met with Alcock several times, Anita Neville more times than I can count, and it's always the same response—it's Martin's decision. All that we have asked for from Martin is a commitment (we don't care how) to make it happen ... During the election campaign, we approached Martin several times to at least come to Winnipeg and make an announcement. We offered the unveiling of the [statue of Mahatma] Gandhi just received from the Indian government and the Chinese railroad worker from the Chinese community, and to make just a statement of support. He declined."

As for Gail Asper, this latest roadblock made her justifiably angry. She wrote to Martin on July 13, 2004, with yet another review of the museum's funding history: "We are deeply disappointed by the comments the Honourable Reg Alcock has recently made wherein he advised that the Government was only committed to $30 million and never made any further commitments. In fact, the announcement of the Museum on April 17th, 2003, was only made after my father received strong assurances from the Liberal Government that the $30 million which was being committed was a first installment and that funding up to $95 million

(or essentially one half of the project) would be found and committed as we raised our $100 million. Mr. Prime Minister, knowing the kind of astute businessman my father was, you must believe us when we say we would never have raised expectations of the public or put so much effort into a project had we not had the assurances of the Federal Government that they were committed to fund 50% of the capital and three quarters of the operating costs of the project."

Subsequent research also revealed that, since 2000, the federal government had spent $1.05 billion on megaprojects in Toronto, including $350 million for the city's transit system and $500 million on the waterfront. In no other area in the country, and certainly not in Winnipeg or even Manitoba, was the federal government spending close to that amount.

Six weeks later, the life-sized statue of Gandhi, created by Ram Vanji Sutar—the gift had been arranged for by Dr. Naranjan S. Dhalla, a distinguished physician and professor of medicine, and a fan of Izzy Asper's—was unveiled at a moving ceremony at the Forks near the site of the CMHR. Besides Babs and Gail Asper, also in attendance were Winnipeg mayor Sam Katz, former mayor Glen Murray, Manitoba MLA Bidhu Jha, and Shashi Uban Tripathi, India's high commissioner to Canada, among others. The most notable guest was, perhaps, Treasury Board president Reg Alcock, who, despite his unhelpful comments some weeks earlier, stated his confidence that "the project would come together."

Solving the federal funding conundrum still remained crucial, especially since the longer there was a delay in beginning construction of the museum, the more likely it was that capital costs would increase. Alcock's renewed optimism aside, the situation looked bleak. A report to Gail from Bob Richardson, a Liberal Party organizer, and Cameron MacKay, a political operative, on September 21 confirmed what

the Aspers already knew. "There is a dearth
of interest in the project beyond Manitoba
MPs," wrote Richardson and MacKay. "Most
Ontario MPs see it as 'a regional play and not as
a national asset.' " Gail and Moe had met several
times with Martin's deputy prime minister,
Alberta MP Anne McLellan. She was not on
board either. "Sources close to the Deputy PM,"
Richards and MacKay noted, "report that she
finds the proposal neither objectionable, nor
overly favourable and thinks that her Western
colleagues feel much the same way. That is to
say that the museum is not off the radar screen,
but it is not a priority."

Three days later, Paul Martin was in Winnipeg to announce that the Public Health Agency
of Canada would be located in Winnipeg. He
decided to stop at Gail Asper's home to speak to
her frankly about the museum. Alcock recalled
that Martin had told him after he had arrived
in the city, "They're going to have to take the
$30 million because that's it."

Once Gail was notified of the meeting, she
ensured she had on hand a bottle of Glenmoran-
gie, a single malt Scotch whisky, Martin's favourite drink. "I was pouring tumblers of it," she
says. She also made a point not to bring up the
sensitive issue of the *National Post* coverage. But
the conversation did not go as Gail had hoped
it would: Martin repeated that the $30 million
was likely all there was for the museum at the
present and that he felt the province and city
could offer more funding.

"It was my brother Leonard again, me, and
Bob McMahon, who was the project manager
at the time doing financial analysis and so on,"
Gail says. "So the prime minister came into my
living room and we had a chat. I actually had
written 'shut up' on my hand because, as you
can tell, I don't ever shut up. Leonard said, 'Gail,
you've got to listen to him. So look at your hand
occasionally and let him speak.' That's when
Martin said, 'Look, this is a lovely project and
a lovely tribute to your father, but considering
this is just a tribute to your dad, $30 million is
more than enough to do something very spectacular. It's very nice you are doing this, but
that's it.' "

Recalling this discussion seven years later
in an interview with the *Winnipeg Free Press,* on
December 24, 2011, Martin disputed the notion
that he opposed the project and suggested that
his hands were tied by federal bureaucrats. "I
supported the museum," he declared, "but . . .
the final decision on the amount was a recommendation from officials." A press report a week
later implied that Martin was insisting that
any further funding be tied to an increase in
the amounts allocated by the province and the
city. It should be stressed, too, as Gail did in her
report of this encounter, that Martin had told
her not to "de-Asperize" the project, "because
one of the reasons he is behind it is because of
Izzy and his respect for him."

Backed into an even tighter corner, and
heeding the advice of others more experienced

in government relations, Gail astutely created an advisory council, which would give further weight to the museum's importance—or so she hoped. Her choice for the chairman of the council was Charles (Charlie) Coffey, a Royal Bank executive who had come to know the Aspers when he spent a few years in Winnipeg in the late 1980s and early 1990s. He was also a Liberal Party supporter with friends in the Martin government. A few weeks into his new assignment, Coffey learned of the strong resistance to establishing a national museum in Winnipeg. The backlash he faced immediately was, he recalled, "Why would anyone go to Winnipeg because of a museum of any kind, let alone a museum for human rights?"

With input from former Liberal MP Patrick Gagnon, Gail and Coffey assembled a council that soon included by any standard an inspiring group of prominent Canadians—former politicians, advisors, professors, business people, ethnic association leaders, a former Supreme Court

judge, and two former prime ministers. Apart from Coffey and Babs Asper, the council by late 2005 consisted of Beth Atcheson, Lloyd Axworthy, Tom Axworthy, Stephen Burri, Patrick Case, Mohinder Singh Dhillon, Frank Dimant, Phil Fontaine, Senator Jerry Grafstein, Rick Hansen, Buzz Hargrove, Andrew Hladyshevsky, Senator Mobina Jaffer, Senator Noël Kinsella, Madam Justice Claire L'Heureux-Dubé, Kathleen Mahoney, Ray McFeetors, Keiko Miki, Ed Morgan, the Right Honourable Brian Mulroney, Senator Vivienne Poy, Victor Rabinovitch, Jean-Guy Rioux, Maurice Strong, Arni Thorsteinson, Alexandre Trudeau, the Right Honourable John Turner, and Rick Waugh.

In the months and years that followed, there would be additions. Also joining the council were acclaimed actor Sir Ben Kingsley (who Gail managed to speak to while he was shooting a film in Winnipeg); Lise Routhier-Boudreau, the president of the Federation of Francophone and Acadian Communities; and Craig Kielburger,

founder of Free the Children. Gail Asper's greatest coup, however, was getting Governor General Michaëlle Jean to act as the museum's honorary patron, along with the lieutenant-governor of Manitoba—first John Harvard in 2009, and then his successor, Philip Lee.

The connection with Jean happened this way: In November 2005, Gail was on her way back from Halifax, where she had received a $100,000 donation from the Government of Nova Scotia. Jean had just been appointed governor general. Gail had heard one of Jean's first speeches and knew she had to have her involved.

Gail called Rideau Hall and made an appointment to speak with the governor general. "I'm on the flight to Ottawa," she remembers, "and, of course, I'm in a white suit and I dump an entire cup of coffee all over me. I go to the cramped bathroom on the plane, and I'm pouring water all over my suit. I end up getting to Ottawa reeking of stale coffee, with this slightly beige-white suit looking so bedraggled and just so pathetic and really feeling tired and out of shape, and my hair's looking awful. But off we go to Rideau Hall. It's like we're in the *Wizard of Oz;* we're going to Emerald City. I walk into Rideau Hall, where I've never been before, and it's so grand and the governor general is so beautiful and so elegant and I'm smelling of coffee. I'll never forget that meeting where I just sat there and pitched her—of course, I did remember the Izzy Asper thing, like how to shut up and not talk for hours . . . She was so gracious and so kind." The governor general told Gail that although she could not raise funds for the museum, she would be honoured to act as patron. "I came out of there just sailing," Gail says. "I couldn't believe that this beautiful and beloved woman who was just revered around Canada was going to be our patron." It was the first honorary patronage the governor general granted.

01/08/2008 05:13 AM

With brand new letterhead listing the names and titles of the esteemed patron and council members, Coffey launched what Gail calls a "massive frenzy; a national campaign of getting articles written and getting many people writing letters to Paul Martin. We asked everybody we knew to write to Paul Martin or write to all the ministers."

Even with the political battle raging, the private sector money kept coming in. Gail Asper's dedicated team running the Friends of the CMHR comprised Kim Jasper, who had been seconded from the United Way to be the Friends' director of communications, and Diane Boyle, who began her work as campaign director in April 2005. "It was," says Jasper, "a wild ride because you were … branding, preparing, promoting, and selling something that didn't exist. It was a vision and it was an idea, and you had to be passionate about the vision to do that." The most common question they heard from

possible donors outside Winnipeg, Boyle adds, was what Gail and Moe also had been repeatedly asked: "Why Winnipeg?"

The constant questioning made the reality of raising funds for the project outside Manitoba a trying exercise, though not an impossible one. It was Manitoba donors, however, who were paramount; by the summer of 2009, for example, the total amount raised from the private sector—five thousand donors in all—exceeded $100 million, with approximately 70 per cent of that total coming from within Manitoba (a ratio that has remained constant).

Still, the money did continue to flow in from a variety of sources. Besides the Winnipeg Foundation and the Buhlers, Canadian banks were the first major corporations to step forward. Both Gail and Moe recall the single most amazing fundraising day they had in Toronto: they met with four of the five major banks in one day and were successful with all of them.

At the end of February 2004, CIBC had donated $1 million, followed by the Bank of Nova Scotia with $1.5 million, the Bank of Montreal with $750,000, and the Royal Bank with $1 million at the end of April. "You have to be persistent," says Gail. "One of the hardest things was I didn't really expect to have to travel so much, and I really regret that I did lose many years of my life with my young family, being on the road constantly, whether it was in Ottawa or going to Toronto, Calgary, Montreal, Halifax, Vancouver, or Edmonton to do fundraisers."

Indeed, the timing of the donations in Winnipeg was not always convenient. CIBC decided to announce its donation on February 15, when Gail was scheduled to be in Whistler, B.C., for a rare and brief family holiday. To get back to Winnipeg for the ceremony, she was forced to "get up at the crack of dawn," as she tells it, charter a helicopter to fly her from Whistler to Vancouver, and then charter a plane to Winnipeg at Asper Foundation expense. She was able

to rejoin her family the next day. If she was frazzled, you cannot tell it from the photograph of her and CIBC CEO John Hunkin that appeared in the newspaper. Balancing family and work was extremely challenging for Gail but remained a priority for her over the years.

Sometimes there were pleasant surprises. "I remember Moe and I went to visit a prospect who owned a trucking company," relates Boyle. "We drove up there, and it was an older rundown building by the railroad tracks. The man was a shoot-from-the-hip-type guy. He had built his business up and was quite brilliant. He was very casually dressed. We just started chatting to him about this project, and he just came out and said, 'Fine, I'll do a million.' We just looked at each other [and said,] 'Okay, thank you.'"

Both Boyle and Jasper agreed that working closely with Gail is an unforgettable experience. "She can drive you crazy because she always sees the things that haven't been done," says Jasper, "but she also praises the things that have been

done well. So no matter how far, how fast, and how quickly you move, there's still more to be done, but that's the challenge of working with her, but it's also the good thing about working her—that 'reach for the stars' attitude. She channels from Izzy every single day. Nothing is ever good enough, and I don't mean that in a disparaging way. It's because we could always do better ... we could always aim higher, and that's, although an exhausting motto, ... a good motto to be mentored under ... She always worked until three or four in the morning. So, you'd always have your light flashing on your phone in the morning. Sometimes there was not a happy voice mail, but she would often phone and sing to me. One voice mail was, 'Kim, I've just been listening to Johnny Cash singing Tom Petty's song, "I Won't Back Down." Here, wait a minute. I'm going to go turn it up, 'Listen, *I won't back down.*' And she'd start singing to me and she said, 'That's the new theme song for the museum. Okay? I won't back down. That's what we're going to sing. Okay, goodbye,' click."

The Friends' secret weapon was the indomitable Babs Asper. She single-handedly obtained a million-dollar donation from Winnipeg automobile dealer Jim Gauthier and his wife, Joyce, who live in the same condominium as she did, and in July 2008 the *Winnipeg Free Press* published a great photograph of Babs and the Gauthier family standing in a Silverado

facing The incredible team behind the Friends of the CMHR. Moe Levy is in the back row, second from right.

top Winnipeg automobile dealer Jim Gauthier and his wife, Joyce, make a generous contribution to the CMHR in July 2008. From L to R: Jim Gauthier, Gail Asper, Babs Asper, Manitoba premier Gary Doer, and Joyce Gauthier.

above Mother and daughter Babs Asper and Gail Asper, the CMHR's most successful fundraisers.

72

with the cheque. For that matter, as Kim Jasper recalls, "People at One Wellington Crescent [where Babs Asper lived] were afraid to go into the elevator for fear that Babs would be there to make a pitch between the floors on the way down to the parking garage or up to their apartments." More than that, she attended every museum event, spoke when invited to do so, raised funds, and provided the Friends with intelligence on whom and whom not to approach. "She was tenacious in pursuing all potential donors, utilizing her amazing ability to balance passionate assertiveness and gentle tact," says Kathy Penner, who joined the Friends in 2007 as its major gifts officer, becoming regional campaign manager for Manitoba and Saskatchewan five years later. Or to put it a different way, "She was great at putting the old Babs squeeze on anyone and everyone," says Moe Levy.

Gail estimates that she has participated in more than fifteen hundred fundraising meetings or calls. And throughout it all she was sustained by humour, music, and the supreme dedication of the team, primarily Moe Levy, Kim Jasper, Diane Boyle, and her mother, Babs. "We were this merry pathologically committed band of foot soldiers, carrying on the vision of our fallen leader that we believed in," she says. "This was never something that was inherited but not accepted. The sense of humour and joie de vivre that we always had made working on the project wonderful even though we were

going through hell much of the time." They commiserated by doing impressions of Monty Python shticks to laugh off the countless rejections and negativity they encountered. One prospect who happened to be in a bad mood tore into them about the project, and after listening to a forty-five-minute tirade, they slunk out of the meeting, dazed. Another who did not like the design of the building kept telling them that they were "losing points" with each utterance. By the time the meeting was over, they reckoned that their score was minus 50. Thereafter, "losing points" became a common reference for a disappointing meeting. And the team had a rule: Gail was permitted to get a manicure only after securing another million-dollar donation.

No one gave up. "There was no room for negativity," Gail asserts. "There was no room for people who didn't believe in the project. The alchemy of successful entrepreneurs does defy reality, defies physics, something does happen. You just do not give up, no matter how many people told us to do so. This museum cost three times more than we expected, but we just raised more money. You never surrender, and you have to adapt to change as the project changes."

During this period, Gail and Moe were on an almost constant shuttle between Winnipeg and Ottawa. "We were the dynamic couple of the Ottawa social scene," says Gail, laughing. In one meeting in early October 2004 with Alex Himelfarb and Martin's chief of staff Tim

Murphy, the same issues that were preventing the flow of money came up again. Gail and Moe were told that the funding was "precedent setting" and that no museum outside Ottawa had ever received such a large amount of money. This "has caused internal issues with other museums," said Himelfarb. The officials repeated Martin's seemingly firm position that more of the funds should come from the province. But the most problematic issue from their perspective was the optics of the deal. "How would Canadians react," they asked, "to spending such a large sum on a museum?"

By January 2005, Alcock informed Gail that he probably could get her another cheque for $30 million, but that would be all. "If we truly want the 'Cadillac version,' we need to continue to work to find a hook to truly engage the prime minister," she suggested in an e-mail to her family. More than once, the Aspers considered scaling back the design of the museum. Yet, in the end, Gail could not do that. "This was

where the Izzy Asper motto 'Reach for the stars' came in," she says. "We were driven, inspired, and haunted by Dad. It had to be iconic. I kept asking myself, 'Why should we goddamn settle?'" And they didn't—but their frustration level was high.

Moe Levy relieved his tension in the pool. "I like to swim," he says. "I normally swim about sixty laps. I came out after this one meeting . . . [and] I was so depressed and I went into the pool and I kept swimming. The lifeguard came and said to me, 'You've been in there for over two hours.' I had done over two hundred laps because I just needed to work it out in some way. It was a very, very trying, very difficult time."

A message to Gail from Alcock near the end of January urged her and Moe to take a step back. "Stay low—for God's sake," Alcock wrote, "do not do anything in Ottawa. Tell Moe to back off. We are real close and the last thing I need right now is any sense that we are pushing. I know that waiting is tough, but trust me for a

few weeks more. I have everything lined up and believe that I can close this soon. If I haven't been successful by mid-March (post budget) then you can call in the dogs. Until then... Shhhhh."

Needless to say, Gail was not sure what to make of this latest directive. "This is a big surprise," she responded to Alcock. "I feel like Charlie Brown and you're Lucy holding the ball. Pushing is exactly what you've said to do!" Alcock replied that he had the situation in hand and that even the ongoing operational funds were still possible. "The problem is that," he added, "support for the project is very fragile. You have significant supporters but you also have significant detractors here in Ottawa and in Toronto."

There was more positive news in February after the federal and Manitoba governments finally settled the matter of the floodway funding and agreed to share the $660-million project. Most significantly, this money was to come from a special national infrastructure fund that would not impede any funding for other provincial projects, such as the museum.

The Juno Awards to honour the best in Canadian music were being held on April 3, 2005, in Winnipeg for the first time, and it seemed too good a national opportunity to pass up. Gail worked diligently behind the scenes so that Kim Jasper's newly designed star lapel pin, a symbol of the museum's and Izzy Asper's "Reach for the stars" motto, would be properly showcased. Gail ensured that everyone from co-host Ben Mulroney on down was wearing one—she had successfully enlisted Ben's father, Brian Mulroney, and a member of the museum's advisory council, in this endeavour. The goal was to show that everyone was wearing a Shine Pin, from the premier and the mayor to the entire staff of the hotel where Liza Frulla, the minister of Canadian heritage, was staying. "We needed Minister Frulla to return to Ottawa reporting that the project was now embraced by everyone," recalls Gail.

The Junos were being broadcast by CTV, but Leonard Asper, the CEO of Canwest Global, decided to host a rival party at which the museum could be showcased. Held in the Wellington Crescent mansion then owned by the Sifton family, the party became the place to go to, thanks in part to a hot house band and the unbelievable venue. The model of the museum was displayed, and all of the guests received Shine Pins, which most of them thought was just a memento of the party. About the only person who refused to wear one was a senior Martin advisor who was in a foul mood, despite the festivities. Asked by a local Young Liberal to don a pin, he said dismissively, "I'm not going to wear this star. I don't like this project, and it's never going to happen."

This advisor was wrong—sort of. Throughout March and early April 2005, Reg Alcock continued to reassure Gail that the capital funding problem would be solved. He was, he said, moving Martin closer to an agreement. By then, Gail and Moe had been trying for about eight months to make an appointment to see Liza Frulla. Nevertheless, Gail soon learned that Alcock had convinced Ralph Goodale, the Liberal finance minister, to support the project, and at long last Martin relented. "The nice thing about Paul is," Alcock said, "if you can make a case for him, [if] you can rationalize a case for him, . . . you can keep coming at him." With plans for the museum to function as a centre for diversity education for both police officers and students, Martin agreed that the CMHR could have the remaining $70 million for its capital costs.

The prime minister telephoned Gail Asper at seven o'clock in the morning on April 15, 2005, to tell her the news. That morning at the Centennial Concert Hall, a crowd of fourteen hundred gathered. First they heard Babs Asper announce that the winner of the architectural competition for his magnificent design for the museum, with its iconic glass tower, was the New Mexico–based architect Antoine Predock. An even bigger surprise came next. Reg Alcock strode onto the stage to proudly state that Jean Chrétien's promise made to Izzy Asper almost two years earlier would be fulfilled. Alcock received a standing ovation.

Gail Asper also informed the delighted audience that a $1-million donation had been confirmed a day earlier from Toronto neurosurgeon Dr. Michael Dan, president of Regulus Investments. This raised the private donations amount to approximately $40 million. It had been a great week in the CMHR's journey. That evening, Gail's husband, Michael, surprised her. He drove her to the museum site at the

Forks, where he presented her with a bottle of champagne. They sipped it while sitting in the vast, empty parking lot they hoped would soon be graced by the world's first human rights museum.

CELEBRATORY CHAMPAGNE notwithstanding—indeed, even before the applause at the Centennial Concert Hall had died down—Gail was still concerned: Alcock's announcement on April 15, 2005, was "really a non-announcement," as Levy dubs it. Here was the crux of the matter: Yes, the museum could have $70 million, provided that Gail and the Friends of the CMHR could raise the required funds and show a business plan that the operating funding was in place. In this classic Catch-22, however, the $15- to $20-million annual operating funds from the government needed to be in place before the project could proceed—and that money was seemingly off the table. In fact, Gail learned some months later that Alcock had sold Martin and the other skeptics in Ottawa on the $100 million by assuring them that they would not have to cover the operating costs.

"The Government's new investment of $70 million is conditional on your securing matching funds from other sources," Judith LaRocque, deputy minister of Canadian heritage, explained in a letter to Gail on April 29, 2005. "The Government of Canada will not be a source of operating funds. The [Asper]

Foundation will therefore need to demonstrate that it has secured adequate funding to operate the museum from other sources."

Not surprisingly, the government's decision, even if it was far from perfect, launched another round of Toronto-based criticism of the project. (Former prime minister Jean Chrétien, on the other hand, told Gail that she had "moved the ball forward down the field. Be gracious, say thanks, and advise everyone who is happy about this development to write and tell this to Prime Minister Martin.") In an April 23, 2005, *Globe and Mail* column, Kate Taylor pointed out the perceived unfairness of the situation. Two museums had closed down in recent months, she wrote, the West Parry Sound District Museum and Quebec's Musée d'art inuit Brousseau, the first public gallery of Inuit art outside the Arctic. An internal report also revealed that the National Gallery in Ottawa had a leaky roof and that museums across Canada were suffering from a lack of funds in general. "Meanwhile, on another planet—well, in Manitoba actually—a proposed human rights museum has just snagged $100 million in federal funding," wrote Taylor, then going on to question the "giddy" design by Predock and why the issue of the operating funds had not yet been resolved.

Two days later, the *Toronto Star*'s Martin Knelman, a former Winnipegger who had attended the Centennial Concert Hall event, responded to carping by Taylor and other

critics. The CMHR, he wrote, "is likely the most thrilling news Winnipeg has had in half a century. Given its mission to draw millions of visitors and tell this country's story to both Canadians and the rest of the world, it should be feted not just in Manitoba but from coast to coast. Instead it has lately become the target of a sneer campaign from the East, especially Toronto, with an outburst of snobbery rooted in the bad old days of mean-spirited Hogtown."

Although Gail and Moe were exhausted, their lobbying efforts to solve the problem of the operating funds continued. Their lives had no structure, and they were constantly on call to fly to Ottawa at a moment's notice for a convention or party where they might be able to speak to a cabinet minister or bureaucrat. If a politician was visiting Winnipeg, they used their contacts to ensure that wherever the visitor went, or whomever they met with, museum Shine Pins would be prominent. It was what Gail calls "the relentless march of the Shine Pins." No visiting dignitary departed from Winnipeg without being impressed that the museum had the vast support of the city and province. Under Charlie Coffey's wise direction, Gail and Moe, along with Kim Jasper and Diane Boyle, approached each government function with a military-like strategy. All Coffey wanted to know after each gathering was, Whom did you speak to? And what did you tell them? "We took professional schmoozing to a new level," says Levy with a smile.

For the next few months, Gail and Moe went door to door, while Reg Alcock sought operating funding support from nearly every federal government department. "But no department had any funds to contribute, we were told," Gail recalls. "At this point, we were absolutely at our wits' end. We were going full steam with all of our governments, and we had a cross-party caucus that was 100 per cent behind the project, and we still couldn't make any headway. This was the darkest, darkest time—I remember a lot of late nights in my kitchen, thinking about my dad. I missed him incredibly. There were a lot of tears, a lot of 'Oh my God, I just lost three years of my life killing myself over this.' And, what troubled me the most was what kind of message were we going to give to Winnipeggers if we, with all of our clout and everything, could not get this thing done." Gail estimates that she and Moe met with more than thirty ministers, deputy ministers, and chiefs of staff to discuss the matter of operating funding.

One strategic tactic on Gail and Moe's part was to point out the unequal nature of federal cultural financial support to the provinces, since the Manitoba government's contribution to the museum remained a sore point for the Martin administration. As Gail drew attention to on many occasions, according to Statistics Canada, Manitoba and Quebec each spent about $96 per capita on culture in 2005; Quebec received $156 per capita from the federal government, whereas Manitoba received only $73 per capita. More questionable was Ontario's funding, which spent $51 per capita on culture but received $119 per capita in federal funding.

None of these reasonable arguments seemed to make much of a difference. As Dan Lett wrote in the *Winnipeg Free Press,* "The Aspers in general, and Gail and Moe Levy in particular, had worn out their welcome in Ottawa." No one in Ottawa wanted to hear anything else about it, Lett added. "Anytime the word 'Asper' was mentioned in Ottawa, eyes would roll back in

their heads[,] like 14 year olds," an unnamed Manitoba official who worked closely on the file told him. "I think the only reason Martin agreed to support it," this individual said, "was that he was afraid of the Canwest media empire. Martin was never receptive to the project."

That attitude was also confirmed in a conversation Gail and Moe had with Alex Himelfarb. As Gail reported to the Asper Foundation board, "He advised that in everyone's mind, when the Government committed to capital money, there was absolutely no expectation whatsoever of any operating money being given. He advises that the inside politicos are angry that they being 'blackmailed.' They do not like this project and none of them have the story as I described it to him, namely that there was always the understanding and the assurance that somehow, not only would capital be put in, but the operating costs would be covered ... None of the PMO or the Cabinet Ministers really understand this, according to Alex. That's because they are impossible to reach, won't meet or return phone calls, so we can't explain the project … Alex reminded us that our advocate and person to keep on board still is very much Reg Alcock and without Alex and Reg, it would have taken many more years to get where we are at."

Gail points to two brief conversations she had during this period that gave her hope. One was with Peter Nicholson, who was then the chief policy advisor in Martin's PMO. "What is it with you guys?" she asked Nicholson in a moment of frustration. His reply was telling. "It is not you, it is the government," he told her. "Get your head out of the sand. There are thousands of people trying to get things done. It's business, not personal." That message convinced Gail that, in Ottawa, it was survival of the fittest.

Another short and meaningful discussion was with Ed Lumley. "Gail, if you want to get anywhere in life," he suggested to her, "you have to be humble, you can't stand on principle, you have to apologize, suck it up, and go and kiss the proverbial ring." These insights from Nicholson and Lumley led to what Gail called "a readjustment of my mindset." She was determined to soldier on with as much passion and commitment as she could muster.

Fate intervened in early November 2005. The Gomery Inquiry's first report was released and the news was not good for the Liberals: although Chrétien and Martin were not held personally responsible, accusations were made about the culpability of Chrétien's chief of staff Jean Pelletier. Martin's attempt to distance himself from his predecessor had backfired. The support of Jack Layton and the NDP for the Liberal minority government collapsed. The Conservatives soon introduced a non-confidence motion, castigating the government for "its culture of entitlement," its "arrogance," and its "corruption." On November 28, the Conservatives' non-confidence motion was supported by the NDP and the Bloc Québécois, and another election was called, for January 23, 2006.

Reg Alcock's campaign literature proudly boasted of his efforts at securing the museum its federal capital funding, which given the conditions attached to the money was in Gail's view a bit of a stretch. "I have covered for Reg since the April 15th announcement 8 months ago and consequently 1.2 million Manitobans believe this project is going ahead," she wrote to Himelfarb early in January. "I am being called to have my photo plastered on all the Liberal candidates' brochures … and I'd like to help them. At the same time, I feel the candidates are campaigning under false pretenses if they state that the Liberals are supporting the Museum, when in fact without any operating funding, the Museum isn't viable and the Federal money won't flow because it's contingent on an approved operating plan, which we don't have without the Federal support. Things are completely out of control—we've been in limbo

79

for nine months and we have limited time and resources to continue to drag this out."

Alcock had one more rabbit up his large sleeve. On January 17, 2006, a week before the election, he wrote to Gail informing her that he had managed to include in the Liberal Party platform—only released on January 11—a promise of potential annual programming funds of about $25 million, which could be accessed by the museum in conjunction with joint education, conferences, and other human rights–related activities between the CMHR, the Global College at the University of Winnipeg, and the Arthur V. Mauro Centre for Peace and Justice at the University of Manitoba. This was not quite the concrete operating funding the museum required, but it was for the moment better than nothing.

To add to the drama, the Aspers chose January 19, 2006, as the date to announce that the Asper Foundation was donating a total of $20 million for the museum—the largest gift the foundation has ever made then or since. Like everyone else in the country, they now awaited the vote three days later to determine if they would still be negotiating with the Liberals or if there would be a new party in charge, as the polls were predicting.

MARTIN AND THE Liberals had run a mediocre campaign. Policy announcements were delayed or not given prominent attention, and owing to the opposition parties, the Gomery Inquiry was always front and centre. Fourteen days before the vote, polls suggested that Harper might win a majority government. Yet, on election day, Canadians were not certain whether they could trust what many perceived to be the Conservatives' extremism, particularly on social issues. Instead, the country got another minority, this time one headed by Stephen Harper, who won 124 of the 308 seats. The Liberals were reduced to 103 and became the official opposition, the Bloc Québécois lost 2 seats for a total of 51, and the NDP gained 9 seats for a total of 29.

Still, any change in government is dramatic. As Gail Asper watched the results unfold on television, she found the Liberal defeat jarring. And among those who lost on January 23, 2006, was the museum's strongest backer, Reg Alcock, who after thirteen years as an MP was defeated in the Winnipeg South riding by a mere 111 votes, losing to Conservative Rod Bruinooge.

Gail was shocked, like every other Liberal supporter in the city. "We see Reg Alcock go down," she recalls. "This was unthinkable. How can Reg Alcock, who was the head of the Treasury Board, the kingpin, lose? I am a Liberal, but I was also kind of intrigued by this whole thing. I thought, *Maybe there's going to be a change here.*"

The future of the Canadian Museum for Human Rights would now be in the hands of Prime Minister Stephen Harper.

05

A SHINING HOUR

STEPHEN HARPER WAS SOLD on the idea of the Canadian Museum for Human Rights well before he moved into 24 Sussex Drive, but he was also troubled by its high costs. The forty-six-year-old prime minister had grown up in Toronto and had relocated to Alberta as a young man. He was educated there, mentored by Preston Manning, the principled crusader and founder of the Reform Party, and was transformed into a westerner in mind and spirit. That grassroots Alberta-based philosophy still resonates today. "The real interest of the Prime Minister appears to lie less in transforming the country's morality and finances," the *National Post*'s Tasha Kheiriddin argued in an April 2012 column, "and more in shifting the geographical axis of power from central to Western Canada."

Thus, building a federal museum outside the National Capital Region was not so huge an intellectual process for Harper, but he still took some convincing. As soon as Gail Asper began communicating with Harper about the

CMHR in 2005, he was interested enough in the project to sit in on Winnipeg Conservative MP Joy Smith's Manitoba caucus meetings, though he was instinctively wary of the high costs the project entailed. Gail tried to allay those concerns. "I have respected your belief in fairness and hope that we can count on your understanding of this principle to support this innovative centre that will not only be a centre [in] which we can finally tell Canadian stories, house our collections, and explain the Charter of Rights and Freedoms," she wrote to him in early February 2005, "but also be the catalyst for the economic rejuvenation of a prairie city."

Gail's relationship with the new prime minister was to grow stronger, but it did not start out that way. In May 2004, during the election campaign, Harper was in Winnipeg and made a snide comment about the high price tag for the $21-million Esplanade Riel pedestrian bridge stretching across the Red River and linking the Forks with St. Boniface. In the middle of the bridge is a restaurant and washrooms that cost upward of $1 million to build. Standing at the foot of the bridge for a photo op, Harper wryly commented, "It's a nice bridge. I wouldn't pay $21 million for it, and I wouldn't pay $1 million for a toilet."

Gail, a Winnipegger from the top of her scarf-covered head to the tips of her fleece-lined winter boots, took umbrage at such a putdown. She fired off a letter to the *Winnipeg Free Press.* "I find Mr. Harper's comments distressing and depressing," she wrote, "because the world he would have us inhabit in Winnipeg would be a far bleaker, uglier one, and I for one believe that the spiritual and economic well-being of Winnipeggers is far better served by placing a value on beauty." Supporters of the museum immediately berated Gail for needlessly antagonizing the would-be prime minister.

Some months later, Harper paid another visit to the city to speak at a Manitoba Progressive Conservative dinner. David Asper, a Harper supporter, arranged a meeting between his sister; his brother, Leonard; and the Leader of the Opposition. Gail wisely apologized for the letter in the newspaper—which she learned, to her dismay, Harper had indeed read and had brought with him—and the three of them then had a fruitful discussion about the museum. Harper was still troubled by the economics of the project, yet appreciated its magnitude. When he became prime minister in January 2006, he agreed without reservation to honour

any federal commitments made by his Liberal predecessors. Hence, the $100-million federal capital contribution was guaranteed. However, the matter of the federal government funding the $15 to $20 million in annual operating expenses was definitely not.

The Aspers' focus was now to establish close links with the Conservative Harper government and to move forward the discussion on the museum's operating funds. Gail Asper and Moe Levy assumed that Vic Toews, Manitoba's new senior Conservative MP, who had been appointed minister of justice, would likely be the politician they could work with. But Toews was not all that interested in the museum, and he gave the file to his colleague, Joy Smith. The Asper Foundation sent Smith a nine-page memo—an "everything you ever wanted to know about the CMHR but were afraid to ask" package—after which, Smith says, "I started to battle for [the museum] long and hard." Working behind the scenes as well was Senator Terry Stratton, who lobbied Harper and assisted Gail and Moe in arranging meetings with the officials in the PMO and various key bureaucrats.

Hence, the Winnipeg-Ottawa shuttle resumed. Still, after more than a month of non-stop travel, Gail was rightly frustrated. She apprised Toews of the situation, knowing her feelings would at least be passed on to the PMO. "After months of meetings and a huge amount of money spent flying back and forth to Ottawa and camping out in hotels and airports, it looks like we have come back with absolutely nothing from any of the departments," she wrote in a letter of February 17, 2006. "Virtually every civil servant told us that they have no budgets for anything to do with the Museum and that until the politicians tell them to find the money, they were not inclined to do so ... Mr. Toews, I am very, very concerned about the future of the project because time is of the essence and if we don't receive any indication of financial support for the operations, we will have to stop the development and disband our team of superb architects, business planners, museum designers, construction managers, human rights experts and capital campaigners. We are moving into a period where we could be spending as much as $700,000 to $800,000 a month in development costs and it would seem foolhardy to do this without any sense of whether this Government supports the concept of contributing towards the operations of the Museum."

There was also the continuing negative campaign by the Canadians for a Genocide Museum to add to her annoyance. On March 6, 2006, the group issued a package and news release calling for Harper to review the "funding of the Asper project" and "to review whether the Asper museum would be 'inclusive and equitable' in its treatments of 'all episodes of genocide that have befouled human history.'" As anyone familiar with the issue understood, this diatribe was merely code for: Would the Holocaust still receive more prominent display and

a larger floor space than the Holodomor? That same day, Moe Levy received a firmly worded letter from Bev Oda, the recently appointed minister of Canadian heritage. It stated, as Levy recalls, "that we had not been flexible in our approach on access to sustainability [operating] funding. We were quite taken aback."

In an attempt to regroup, Levy composed a long letter to Oda's deputy minister, Judith LaRocque, reviewing everything that had transpired over the past two years. Meanwhile, Gail continued to lobby for a meeting with Harper and pointed out to anyone who would listen—including advisory council member Brian Mulroney, who had the ear of the prime minister—that, on a per capita basis, annual federal cultural spending in Manitoba amounted to $100 million less than what was spent in Quebec on an annual basis. "That's a heck of a lot of museums, galleries, festivals, and artistic activity," she told Mulroney. Still, Oda, LaRocque, and other officials were not as bowled over by this fact as were Gail and Moe. As each meeting failed to produce the results they hoped for, they would trudge from Parliament Hill back to the Château Laurier hotel to find some solace at the hotel's bar with a bottle of red wine.

It was primarily a result of David Asper's connections and Joy Smith's diligence that the hoped-for meeting with the new prime minister finally took place on March 21, 2006, in Ottawa. Gail, Moe, and David Asper sat down for a critical discussion with Harper, Smith, and

LaRocque. Gail's recollection of the meeting is positive. "We thoughtfully made the case about the economic benefits," she says. "I had all of my stats in line about the funding the province had given us and what the federal government had given Manitoba." At the conclusion of the meeting, Gail continues, "Harper said, 'I will let you know what the options are,' and he turned to Judith LaRocque and said, 'I want to know what my options are.' And I said, 'Well, when would we have an answer?' And he said, 'We'll have an answer by springtime.' So that was March, and I'm thinking, 'Okay, in May we'll have some answer.'"

That's not what happened. There is no doubt that many civil servants believed the Harper government would not last, so procrastination on the museum file may have seemed to be a sensible policy. Once she returned to Winnipeg, Gail wrote a heartfelt letter to the prime minister reviewing the discussion, and then, channelling her father, added, "What concerns me most as a citizen of Manitoba is that we have stopped daring to dream—we come from a background of accepting mediocrity, of cynicism, of self-effacement and self-denigration . . . We have a new coach, Prime Minister—you. We have a team ready to keep playing and ready to win, so I do hope that you can find the time to hold the baby or coach the team or whatever other analogy or mixed metaphor appeals to you."

In the body of that letter was an even more critical comment: "We always envisioned the Museum as a subsidiary of the National Museum of Civilization and a sister to the War Museum. We would readily revert to the original proposal and transfer control of the project to the Federal Government. Our role would become similar to that of the National Gallery's Foundation, which led by Tom D'Aquino as Chair, plays a strong fundraising role which augments the operating revenues of the National Gallery. And, yes, that would mean relinquishing decisions over architecture, content and governance to the Federal Government, which we would be prepared to do." Much to Gail's chagrin, deciphering the full implication of these words would become the focus of the seemingly endless and frequently infuriating discussions for the next year.

AFTER ANOTHER LONG and cold winter, the snow melted in Winnipeg, always a pleasant event in the city. Week after week, Gail and Moe kept a close eye on the mail, fax machines, and computer screens for a sign that Ottawa knew they were still alive. "There was nothing," Gail says. "March goes by and not a letter requesting information. April goes by, then May. We said, 'Look, we've got to find out what's going on. Why are we not hearing anything?'" Gail had hoped that a decisive announcement of a deal could be made at the Forks on April 17, 2006, the third anniversary of the initial gathering about the museum, which Izzy had hosted, and the anniversary of the Charter of Rights and Freedoms. It didn't happen.

On the other hand, the money from private sources, mainly from generous Manitobans, continued to roll in at a steady pace. Nearly $7 million in donations had been pledged in December 2005 from Bob and Cathy Tallman, the Pollard family, a private family foundation from Vancouver, and an anonymous donor from Winnipeg. That was followed in 2006 with three million-dollar gifts each from Gerry Gray and his family; Richard Morantz and his

wife, Sheree Walder Morantz; and the Kahanoff Foundation of Calgary; $500,000 from Sandy and Debbie Riley, and $3 million from the ever reliable Richardsons. By the beginning of 2007, the Friends had raised close to $70 million, of which about 70 per cent had been donated by Manitobans. And, as 2007 began, Gail received one of the most wonderful surprises: an unsolicited gift of $1 million from Bob Harris, the owner of R.S. Harris Transport. In a rather uncharacteristic description of herself, Gail commented to the *Winnipeg Free Press* on February 6, 2007, "I just was speechless." This donation was soon followed by yet another $1 million from Leo Ledohowski, the president and CEO of Canad Inns.

In the end, this incredible support impressed Stephen Harper. "This community moved forward," as he later put it, "and laid the groundwork for creating something here with an enormous amount of its own resources." How could he as prime minister ignore this remarkable generosity and endorsement of a museum by the community and nearly every politician in Manitoba, regardless of what party they represented? The answer was that he could not, but figuring out a comprehensive and agreeable solution wasn't easy. By the beginning of May 2006, Gail had reluctantly taken a step back—at least that's what she told Jason Kenney, who was then Harper's parliamentary secretary. "The funding process has been so mind-boggling challenging that I don't think we could possibly be more challenged," she said, "and we're simply learning to accept the fact that everything takes much more work and takes much longer to get done than we imagined (kind of like remodeling my kitchen). Fortunately, I worked with my father for 14 years and learned that perseverance is omnipotent (in the words of Calvin Coolidge). It may take 10 years to do something that we thought should take one year, but if the vision is sound and the will is there, anything is possible."

A few weeks later, it was clear from discussions with Bev Oda that the federal government was not prepared to offer the operating money. A decision had to be made as to whether to take the $100 million and use it as an endowment. The revenues from that could be used to fund the operating costs. Or the museum could become a federal institution, with the Asper Foundation's contribution of $20 million, but with control of the museum in the hands of a government body. By this time, almost $7 million of Asper money had been spent, with no firm decision by the federal government. The Friends of the CMHR had also warranted that should the project not proceed, all funds raised from private donors would be redirected to a charity of those donors' choice. Only Asper money was used and at risk at the front end.

To her credit, Gail, backed by her mother, stubbornly stuck to her plan and was not ready to capitulate. She fired off another letter to Harper on May 23, thanking him one more time for seeing her two months earlier and fishing for news of any advancement in their discussions. A week later, Gail was in a meeting with a group of Winnipeg businessmen and representatives from the province and the city when she received a telephone call from Bev Oda. It was a two-minute conversation, but the gist of it was that the federal government was willing to look at the option of making the CMHR a federal institution.

Another month went by. Then, late in the afternoon on Friday, June 30, just before the start of the Canada Day long weekend, the Asper Foundation received a fax from Ottawa. The three-page letter was from Judith LaRocque and laid out the options. The first was for the museum to accept the $100 million, and that would be the end of federal involvement. This was an option Gail had already rejected. The second had more potential.

"The CMHR," LaRocque explained, "would be established as a national museum through an amendment to the Museums Act. You have suggested that one approach might be for the Foundation to complete the building and then transfer it to the Government of Canada. This approach would require further consideration by the government. Since the Government would, in this scenario, have the ongoing responsibility to operate the completed building and set programs, it would wish to be fully engaged in consideration of the proposed design and manage the construction project." To that end, LaRocque asked for an update report with all relevant data—everything from information on land surveys and fundraising to parking spaces and sewage plans.

So much for the long weekend. Over the next ten days, the requested material was gathered together in several boxes and shipped off to Ottawa. All the while, Gail, Moe, and the other trustees of the Asper Foundation sought to determine if there was still a way to make the museum a national institution while preserving some control over its design and content. "When Minister Oda suggested that the Museum could possibly be a national institution," Gail wrote to LaRocque on July 11, "we envisioned something similar to the Canadian International Grains Institute where a multi-million-dollar annual investment by the Government of Canada supports an international education initiative, program initiative and technical exchange program. In fact, we have researched this initiative and believe it holds many similarities to the Museum and would not create an unwieldy precedent for the Government of Canada to implement."

More talks were held through the summer, although it was clear—that is, to everyone but Gail Asper—that if the museum was to become a federal institution, the federal government would assume complete and total control over it. On October 6, the foundation flew out its entire team to Ottawa, along with representatives from the Friends, the architect of record,

construction managers, and museum staff members who already had been hired, for a full day of discussions with LaRocque and Canadian Heritage officials. The meeting was productive, but yet again weeks went by without another word. In the meantime, the Asper Foundation trustees had voted unanimously to support the creation of a federally controlled CMHR under the Museums Act. In a letter of October 30 to Harper, Gail politely urged the prime minister to have the matter resolved by the cabinet before the end of November so that the relationship between the Friends (and the private funds the organization had raised) and the federal government could be determined.

Reviewing this letter, David Asper felt that Gail had not yet fully accepted the ramifications of federal control. "The interim period (the next 12 months) is going to have to reflect the direct involvement by the feds, and like it or not they are going to have the right to evaluate the fundraising progress," he wrote to his sister in an e-mail. "All your talk here about handing it over once it's developed and completed, in my humble view, that is not going to fly. Neither is vitiating the feds' rights to appoint directors. The board is a government board now and the government will control it." As this process wound its way through another month, it was clear that Gail and the Friends were going to have to agree to raise money for a museum for which they would not have the final say. "This does not mean they [the federal government] won't necessarily appoint members of [the] Friends to the Board," David added in another lucid memo, "but it is pretty clear that the Feds will run the show in all respects in that scenario. As we have discussed, this means you will be raising money toward a museum over which you may not have control over the design and no control over the exhibits if it is a federal institution."

Gail accepted her brother's accurate diagnosis of the situation and matters continued to move forward in December 2006. Harper and Doer met in the middle of the month and agreed on a timetable for a joint announcement, possibly in February. At the same time, Gail e-mailed Kevin Lynch, who had replaced Alex Himelfarb as clerk of the Privy Council and secretary to the cabinet, expressing what had now become her standard plea: "We appreciate that the wheels of government do not always move as fast as we would all like, but this matter is significant and the cost to us in the millions of dollars, which I then have to fundraise," she wrote. "Kevin, please get us out of this bureaucratic spiral and get us the appropriate Cabinet approval so we can move ahead."

In fact, the "bureaucratic spiral" dragged on for another four long months, until at long last an acceptable agreement was hammered out. Later in a feature article about the museum published in the *Winnipeg Free Press* on December 24, 2011, Dan Lett suggested that Moe Levy—in a process Manitoba officials caustically referred to as being "Levied"—kept demanding innumerable

changes to the document, and even allegedly faxed a new set of demands right from Doer's office without the premier or his staff's knowledge. Levy scoffs at such an accusation, pointing out that the suggestion that he had such access to the premier's office is ludicrous.

Lett's story had one thing right, however: the negotiations consumed Gail, Moe, and government officials for weeks. Harper made his intentions known to Gail in a letter at the beginning of February 2007, setting the tone for what ensued during the next few months. "It is important that there be a clear understanding of what would be involved if the CMHR were to become a national museum as well as of the respective roles of the Government and the Friends Foundation," the prime minister wrote. "These requirements are not subject to negotiation, as they flow from policies and legislation that govern such undertakings in the interests of accountability and sound management of public funds on behalf of all Canadians." And that meant that the federal government would assume responsibility for all aspects of the museum—its design, construction, exhibits, programming, and content.

Harper still wanted to proceed carefully and was concerned about the museum's budget and the scale of the project. One day in March 2007, David Asper, who was then completing his master of laws at the University of Toronto, received a telephone call from Ray Novak, at the time Stephen Harper's principal secretary (and

currently his chief of staff), inviting him to a meeting at a downtown Toronto hotel. Without hesitation, David cut out of his class and headed to the hotel. Waiting for him there was the prime minister, who wanted to review the proposed terms of the draft CMHR–federal government agreement, as well as issues Asper had raised in a recent memo to Harper. As David remembers, Harper "outlined where they were headed and asked if I thought it met our needs. I advocated for one or two items that I thought weren't particularly contentious, and I do recall that he agreed with whatever we were talking about. He wanted to know that I would support the direction in my dealings with the family, and I assured him I would." David also told the prime minister that he had no doubt that his sister, Gail, was determined to raise the funds required in order to fulfill the complete vision of the museum and not have it compromised. David Asper departed the meeting with the view that he had put Harper's mind at ease.

Indeed, soon after, a "Statement of Intent" miraculously was agreed to in principle and signed on April 20, 2007, by the federal government, the Friends of the CMHR, the governments of Manitoba and Winnipeg, and the Forks Renewal Corporation. It had taken four difficult, almost impossible, years, but the conundrum of the capital and operating costs seemingly had been settled. The agreement laid out the financial commitments and obligations of the various parties completing the museum. Most important, it reflected the right of the Friends to have representation on the CMHR board, and required the board to give due consideration to the architectural design of Antoine Predock and Ralph Appelbaum's master exhibit plan.

That day, Harper flew to Winnipeg to make the official announcement before a standing-room-only crowd of CMHR supporters at the Fairmont Winnipeg hotel, including the members of the Asper family. "This museum," declared the prime minister, "the realization of

Izzy Asper's vision, will celebrate and promote awareness of human rights in Canada, and it will bring Canadian and international visitors to Winnipeg so they can see and hear the Canadian human rights story." There were cheers and applause all around. In honour of her father and his dream, Gail made a point of having Izzy Asper's favourite drink—a gin martini with a splash of vermouth, olives, and ice.

The *Winnipeg Free Press*'s front-page headline the next day, "Izzy Asper's Dream Lives," summed up the moment nicely, and the paper's editorial gave it the necessary perspective. "The museum is arguably the most important development project in the city's history," the editorial began. "The floodway provides protection and the aqueduct delivers our drinking water, but neither of them—important as they are—compares to the museum as a source of inspiration and pride for Winnipeggers. In addition to creating thousands of construction jobs and hundreds of full-time jobs, it will be a national

and international destination, particularly for students from across Canada, who will receive funding to attend its programming. Soldiers, police officers and foreign-service workers will also benefit from its programs on human rights. The spinoff benefits will be enormous, with a heightened sense of confidence being the most important of them all."

The only losers in all of this, as columnist Dan Lett suggested, were the Liberals, who had helped launch the project in 2003, promised the $100 million in federal funding, and then permitted bureaucratic wrangling to delay it interminably—despite the diligence of Reg Alcock, who did everything he possibly could to cut through the red tape. Yet, it was the Liberals "who used the museum as fodder in a pointless clan war over the leadership of the party," Lett wrote about the Chrétien-Martin feud. "It was the internal battle that ultimately cost the Liberals any applause for having ever supported the project."

A WEEK AFTER the hoopla died down, Gail wrote Harper to thank him once more for the "extraordinary announcement" about the CMHR. "When I heard you explaining the vision for the museum, I knew we were in superb hands and that you really understood the overall concept of and need for the museum." Ever the diplomatic politician, Gail took the opportunity to address the tricky matter of the CMHR's governance. "I hope I'm not jumping the gun here," she continued, "but I thought it would be advisable to share my views with regard to the governance structure, the hiring of the CEO and content which is required to ensure the Canadian Museum for Human Rights is successful in all its facets."

Gail's vision was for a strong first-class board that was representative of "the country geographically and is respectful of gender and visible minority balance" and that would include members with diverse backgrounds in business, marketing, tourism, history, and education, as well as experts in human rights. "Above all," she stressed, "we will need a board of directors of people who are not there just to fill a space, but who are actually willing to roll up their sleeves and turn their minds to taking the museum from being simply a building with stories and artifacts to an international education and action centre, which can have impact globally." To her letter she attached a list of ninety-eight people the government might want to consider. Tellingly, of those on Gail's list, only Vancouver

chartered accountant Lisa Pankratz is currently on the CMHR's Board of Trustees, although another recommendation, Bill Barkley, the former CEO of the Royal B.C. Museum, did serve a term, and Arni Thorsteinson, who worked with Izzy in the creation of Canwest, served as the first chair of the board.

Gail had equally high hopes for the museum's CEO, for which a search had already commenced. "The CEO," she wrote, "must have impeccable global connections so that the museum becomes the automatic go-to place for international human rights events. It goes without saying that the CEO must have superb public speaking, networking and communication skills because I also envision this person attending events like the Clinton Global Initiative or even Davos (if invited) where outstanding connections can be made not only for financial support, but for partnership opportunities such as exchanging exhibits, and attracting internationally renowned speakers to the museum."

Finally, Gail urged Harper to review Ralph Appelbaum Associates' proposed exhibit design, which had been meticulously researched and developed for the past three years, at considerable expense. "Once the Government understands what we have developed," she explained, "it would appreciate the importance of the need for there to be a balance between this being an artifact based museum...and an interactive idea museum, which is a new concept for current museum planners."

There was still much to do on the project—not the least of it being for Gail and the Friends to raise an additional $30 million in private funding before construction on the estimated $265-million museum could start—but she closed her letter by expressing her confidence to Harper that "since we're all on the same page, we will work together to make the Statement of Intent a Definitive Agreement."

Lest Gail have any doubts about relinquishing control of the museum to the federal government (which she did not), Judith LaRocque made things plain. "After the Prime Minister had done the announcement of the Statement of Intent, [LaRocque] said to me, 'Gail, I want you to understand something perfectly clearly. You owe this museum completely 100 per cent to Stephen Harper. Don't ever forget that'—meaning that if it had been up to her, there would have been no way they would have set this precedent. And to be fair to Judith, this was just going to be one big headache for her because when you start up with a national museum in Winnipeg, where was it going to end?"

IN ANOTHER LETTER Gail sent Harper, on April 26, she added more words of thanks, encouragement, and optimism. "While no one can deny that we hit a few perfect storms with the museum project over the last six years," she wrote, "I definitely see smooth sailing from here on in." She should have known better.

There was yet more carping from the *Globe and Mail* about Harper's decision when Ralph

Appelbaum unveiled the master exhibit plan at a news conference held at the Winnipeg convention centre. In a May 5, 2007, column entitled "A Winnipeg Museum: Will Anyone Come?" Val Ross wondered, "Does Stephen Harper know what he's letting out of the box? Did he intend Ottawa's support for the Canadian Museum for Human Rights to help it host debates over the rights of, say, Afghan prisoners?" For better or worse, the CMHR, Ross conceded, could be "a lightning rod for controversy … if it does its job."

The smooth sailing Gail had predicted proved to be slightly rougher over the duration of 2007. The governance of the museum also continued to be a matter of much discussion, since Gail wanted to ensure that the Friends of the CMHR and the Manitoba government were properly represented on the board.

Meanwhile, Gail, Moe, and Babs Asper, along with the Friends, were battling to raise the required private money so that construction of the museum could finally begin. By the end of September, the first draft of the Definitive Agreement had been written and another round of back-and-forth negotiation ensued. All the while, as Gail told Kevin Lynch on November 12, construction costs were rising. "For every month the project is delayed, the costs will increase by $1.3 million," she estimated. Since the various governments were not going to offer any more funding, this meant that the onus would be on her and the Friends to raise even more money to make up the shortfall. Nonetheless, officials at the Department of Canadian Heritage moved at their own exasperating pace.

Another twelve weeks went by before the agreement was ready for cabinet approval. That was given on February 7, 2008. The next hurdle was for Bill C-42, An Act to Amend the Museums Act, to pass through the House of Commons and the Senate, and to then receive royal assent so that the CMHR could receive federal funds for its operations. Anticipating these developments, by January 2009, Gail and Moe had been busy ensuring that the bill would receive unanimous consent in the House. If it did not, the bill would have to be referred to a parliamentary committee. Their greatest fear was that it could get bogged down with community consultations that could take months, if not years, and as had happened in the past with the Canadian War Museum's proposed Holocaust gallery, this bill would then have died. And with the possibility of an election being called, "this whole process could get derailed," as Gail reported to the Asper Foundation on February 8. (In fact, the election Gail and Moe feared did not take place until October 14, 2008, and Harper and the Conservatives maintained their minority government.)

Working closely with Émilie Potvin, the chief of staff for Josée Verner (who had replaced Bev Oda as minister of Canadian heritage in the summer of 2007), Gail and Moe were assured on several occasions that everything was under control. "They kept telling us to do nothing, which was very worrying" Gail recalls.

"Anytime anybody has told us to do nothing and wait, we've done the opposite . . . In hockey, the minute a team stops moving they get scored on, but if you keep moving, you make a play. We were always moving. We never would stop doing something."

However, Moe was suddenly advised that it was going to be his and Gail's responsibility to get unanimous consent for the bill after all, and that they would need to work with the three opposition parties to do so. But there was a catch. They had only three days before the bill got introduced, on February 11—thus, a Friday and a weekend—to put it in place. The reason for this short window of time was that the government wanted to introduce the bill without lengthy debate. If all parties agreed and there was unanimous consent, the bill would be approved. Over a few days, Moe, through his connections, managed to get Richard Marceau, a former Bloc Québécois MP, to meet with Bloc leader Gilles Duceppe to obtain his endorsement. Levy also worked with Pat Martin of the NDP, who spoke to the party leadership and was advised that as long as this was a stand-alone bill, they would support it. Gail enlisted the support of Manitoba Liberal MPs Anita Neville and Raymond Simard to ensure all-party support. Simard was completely briefed on the Bloc's position. He and Gail also spoke to several MPs who they thought might not follow party lines. By the end of the weekend, Gail and Moe were confident that the three opposition parties, the Liberals, NDP, and the Bloc Québécois, were on board.

Josée Verner introduced the bill on February 11, 2009, and it was given first and second readings—so far, so good. Two days later, it was scheduled for the crucial third and final reading. As is recorded in Hansard, the verbatim transcripts of parliamentary debates, the Conservative government's house leader, Peter Van Loan, rose and said to the Speaker of the House, Peter Milliken: "Mr. Speaker, I believe that there have been consultations among the parties and there is consent for the following motion: That, notwithstanding any Standing Order or usual practices of this House, Bill C-42, An Act to Amend the Museums Act and to make consequential amendments to other acts shall be deemed to have been read a second time and referred to a committee of the whole, deemed considered in committee of the whole, deemed reported without amendment, deemed concurred in at the report stage, and deemed read a third time and passed."

To this Milliken asked, "Does the Honourable government House leader have the unanimous consent of the House to propose the motion?" Van Loan believed he did. Everyone in the House shouted "Agreed," except one lone member of the Bloc, Michel Guimond, who yelled "No."

Raymond Simard, who had been guaranteed by Moe Levy several times in the past few days that the Bloc MPs were going to unanimously support the bill, was shocked. "I'm thinking, *What the heck's going on here?*" he recounts. "The

one thing about the Bloc, when they give you their word that they're sticking with you, they won't change it. You may not agree with their philosophy, but in terms of those guys being straight shooters, they're usually straight."

Peter Van Loan was also stunned. Immediately, Simard walked over to speak with Guimond. He recalls the tense conversation as follows: "'Michel, you voted on the wrong deal. You voted against us, you should have been supporting this.' He says to me, 'No, no, I know what I voted on.' I said, 'Michel, look at this. Look at it more carefully.' So we started looking through his papers, and in the end he said, 'Oh my God, I did vote against it.' So I said, 'Michel, if I talk to the other parties, if I go see the Speaker, are you prepared to stay here and vote for this right now?' He said, 'Absolutely I am.' It was just an error."

Simard spoke to Van Loan and the NDP members, who all agreed to a re-vote. He approached Peter Milliken. "Mr. Speaker," he said. "I think if you tried this again, we might get it through this time." Milliken asked, "Are you sure?" And Simard replied, "Well, I think, I'm almost positive." Milliken agreed to the re-vote.

Van Loan stood again. "Mr. Speaker, I will try this again. I am pleased to report that there have been further consultations among the parties. This time I will give it a try in the other official language in order to be totally clear." And he repeated what he had moved the first time, but in French. "Does the Honourable Leader of the Government in the House of Commons have the unanimous consent of the House to propose this motion?" asked Milliken again. The honourable members all agreed. "The House has heard the terms of the motion. Is it the pleasure of the House to adopt the motion?" Milliken asked. "Agreed," the members declared. It was done.

Back in Winnipeg, Moe Levy was beside himself. He had received an e-mail at 2:15 PM informing him that the bill had not received unanimous consent. Gail Asper, who was in the middle of a Great-West Life audit meeting, received a telephone call from Anita Neville, saying that she was sorry: they had tried, but the Bloc had voted it down. Gail's heart sank like a stone. Then, an hour later, Moe received a voice mail from Ralph Goodale. "Mr. Levy, it's about 3:30 Ottawa time on Wednesday afternoon. I think Anita Neville and Ray Simard have been in touch with you about Bill C-42. There was a bit of a procedural mistake made in the House earlier today by the Bloc Québécois, but I just wanted to let you know that the Liberals were cooperating with the motion all the way through. After the Bloc Québécois made a mistake, Ray Simard and Anita Neville got them all straightened out. The matter was reconsidered and the bill was passed . . . I just wanted to reassure you that the Liberals were supportive all the way through and particularly in the last minute when the Bloc Québécois got confused."

It was extremely important that Ray Simard was there . . . [and] got them back on track, and ultimately Bill C-42 was passed [unanimously]." Moe's sigh of relief might have been heard all the way back to Ottawa. "No doubt," Levy rightly informed everyone involved, "Ray Simard was the hero of the day!" An hour later, Gail called Simard on his cellphone to thank him.

The bill was finally forwarded to the Senate, where Rod Zimmer, who had worked with Izzy Asper in the early 1980s, supported by Mira Spivak, a long-time friend of the Asper family, and Terry Stratton, an ardent supporter, among others, ushered it through another three readings. "Honourable senators," said Zimmer during the second-reading debate, "if you were to glance up in the gallery today, you might be able to picture Izzy smiling proudly down upon us, because I hope his dream is about to come true." Zimmer did not have to wait long. The bill was discussed in the Senate's Standing Committee on Human Rights before it was back for a third reading on March 5. That vote, too, as in the House of Commons, passed unanimously. "Incredible!" declared Babs Asper when she got the news from Zimmer. "Words cannot express our appreciation. We'll have to mark this date for an annual celebration." Levy immediately received a call from Stratton: "We just passed Bill C-42; your museum has gone through the Senate and has been approved in three readings, so all that's now left is royal assent."

That should have been straightforward, but it was not. A day later, Stratton called Moe again. "Just to give you an update, the government for some strange reason is not intending to [send it for royal assent] until the end of next week ... So my concern of course is, the way things are right now, the government could fall. I think it would be appropriate if some phone calls could be made to the appropriate people because this could be done by written assent; you don't need the GG in the chamber to do this. So my advice to you: try to put pressure on the government to get this done by written consent as soon as possible." Moe did just that. In a few days, he managed to write to every senator and advise him or her of the need for support. He received several very positive comments in return.

At long last, Bill C-42 received royal assent a week later, on March 13, 2008. "A star has been born," Gail told the *Winnipeg Free Press* from Ottawa where she, Moe Levy, and Kim Jasper had travelled to witness the signing first-hand. "It's a beautiful thing for all of Canada and for the world." The happy trio from Winnipeg were photographed standing in front of the Parliament Buildings toasting the news with martinis—as Izzy Asper might have. Both Babs and Gail said independently of one another that Izzy's first comments about this would have been "What took you so long?" Added Babs, "I wavered sometimes, but with Gail and everybody behind it, I knew we'd get here. It just took a little longer than we thought."

99

Premier Gary Doer was equally thrilled. "I always thought the political will would trump the kind of institutional bureaucratic inertia to keep everything in Ottawa," he said. "It will be a beacon of celebrating the triumphs of humans to protect human rights over the intolerance of our national history, and the hate in the world."

UPON THEIR RETURN to Winnipeg, it was back down to earth for Gail, Moe, Kim, and the rest of the Friends. There were some big decisions to make over the next year in anticipation of the start of construction in 2009. Millions more had to be raised from the private sector, and discussions started at once over the termination of the Friends' advisory council and the creation of the CMHR's new Board of Trustees. "I think it's time to get re-involved," Gail asserted in June 2008, "and make sure that the most important decisions in the life of the museum are not botched because [people] are too busy to focus on them and others who want to impose power are using their muscle and interest to gain ground."

In fact, things were advancing. On March 31, 2009, Josée Verner received a seventy-seven-page report on the museum's mandate and operations from a heritage advisory committee she had established in October 2007. This group consisted of Arni Thorsteinson, a member of the Friends' advisory council and a long-time friend and business associate of the Asper family, who served as chair; Gail Asper; Bill Barkley, the former head of the Royal B.C. Museum; Benoît Bouchard, a former Conservative cabinet minister and ambassador to France; Constance Glube, a former chief of the Supreme Court of Nova Scotia; Mary Gusella, a career federal public servant; Vim Kochhar, a Toronto businessman (who was appointed as the first Indo-Canadian to the Senate in 2010); architect John Petersmeyer; and Jonathan Vance, a professor of history at the University of Western Ontario.

Most important, and in line with Gail's earlier position, the heritage committee in its report to Verner urged that the government adopt a policy of "autonomous governance" so that "the integrity and balance of its exhibitions and programs" were not "influenced by political activities or special-interest groups." The report recommended as well the appointment of a

content advisory committee as "an independent group of human-rights scholars, specialists and leaders . . . to elicit information from individuals, organizations and groups." In fact, this had already been done by the Friends in late 2005 with the creation of its Content Advisory Committee, headed by lawyer and human rights advocate Yude Henteleff. It was essential, too, the heritage committee wrote, for the CMHR board "to develop a policy and strategic plan of national engagement at the outset, to ensure that the museum remains focused on its programs to all Canadians and visitors."

At the end of August, Verner, with much input from David Penner of Harper's PMO,

named the CMHR's first Board of Trustees. The decision had been made with due consideration and she had come up with an accomplished group of individuals representing all corners of the country. Several had been members of her advisory committee, including Arni Thorsteinson, who retained his role as chair on the new Board of Trustees; Gail Asper; Bill Barkley; Constance Glube; and Vim Kochhar. They were joined by Montreal businessman Ronald Corey, the former president and chief of operations of the Montreal Canadiens; Yves Laberge, a prolific professor of philosophy and sociology at Université Laval, in Quebec City, and a museum consultant; and Wilton Littlechild, a lawyer from Alberta who had been the first indigenous person admitted to Queen's Counsel by the Alberta Law Society and had served as a Conservative MP from 1988 to 1993. In 2009, the government announced two additional appointments to the board, both with financial experience: Eric Hughes, a financial officer at Wave Energy in Alberta, was appointed as vice-chairman of the board; and accountant Lisa Pankratz, the president and chief compliance officer of Mackenzie Cundill Investment Management, was appointed as a new trustee.

The board held its inaugural meeting in Winnipeg on September 3, 2008. Gail Asper was pleased. "This was truly an historic moment in Canada's history," she wrote to Stephen Harper, "the first board meeting of a national museum created outside the Capital region and only the fifth since Confederation... While some of the board members were familiar to me from our work together on the Minister of Canadian Heritage's Advisory Committee for the Museum, it was a pleasure meeting the other new board members. I think the commitment, expertise and energy of this group is phenomenal. Having sat on many boards over the years, I was most impressed by the high level of experience, common sense and passion for the subject matter. Although this year will require an extraordinary amount of hard work from all of the Trustees, I know we are up to the challenge and eager to move forward."

This productive collaboration aside, Gail and the other trustees were more preoccupied with the museum's rising construction budget. By the end of October, the $200-million museum envisaged by Izzy Asper in 2001 had increased to $310 million—more than $45 million above the last projection of $265 million that everyone had been using for the past two years, and the number on which the Definitive Agreement was based. The budget, as Moe Levy explained to Gary Doer, was based on the construction starting in February 2009, as well as on bringing the structure up to the specifications of LEED, a green building rating system. Levy was seeking an additional contribution of $6.71 million by the province, which had already increased its funding to $40 million, together with top-ups from the federal government ($17 million), the City of Winnipeg ($3.25 million), and private funding ($18 million).

Predictably, no level of government was anxious to comply with the request. In May 2009, Doer said that the province might offer more money for the museum's multimedia display, but in the end no extra funding was allocated. The federal government would not go beyond the $100 million it had committed, a position made perfectly clear when the CMHR budget was tabled in the House of Commons in mid-May 2009. "Our government is contributing $100 million towards the construction of the museum and will assume operating costs of approximately $21.7 million a year," said Deirdra McCracken, spokeswoman for Canadian Heritage Minister James Moore, who had taken

101

over from Josée Verner in October 2008. "This will be the extent of the federal government's financial contribution." It also took another two years, until April 2011, before Winnipeg mayor Sam Katz announced that the city agreed to provide the museum with an additional $3.6 million in funding, redirecting money the city received from the federal government in civic taxes.

The responsibility for the additional $45 million fell on the collective shoulders of the Friends, and the private-funding campaign continued unabated into the new year. There were gifts of $1 million from the Carolyn Sifton Foundation, the Assembly of Manitoba Chiefs, and the South Beach Casino & Resort; $250,000 from the Canadian Union of Public Employees; and $225,000 from Winnipeg Realtors. But that

was only part of the story. In 2009 and ever since, despite continuing criticism from some quarters about the museum's high costs and questions about its content, the CMHR captured the imagination of Canadians, and Winnipeggers in particular, and dozens of businesses, organizations, student groups, and individuals acting on their own held rallies and fundraising events to support it. By the spring of 2009, the Friends' fundraising efforts exceeded

$100 million. Soon after it was constituted, the CMHR's board realized that further delay would only increase costs, and so it approved Predock and Appelbaum's designs, and asked management to begin development.

The museum was going ahead as planned.

06

DESIGNING A DREAM

THE FIERCE COMPETITION among the world's five dozen leading architects from twenty-one countries on five continents to win the contract for building the Museum for Human Rights in Winnipeg was unprecedented in the annals of Canadian architecture. When the original call for entries went out soon after Izzy Asper's death in October 2003, some 530 architects from all over the world, including Iran and the United Arab Emirates, considered the project. "We were getting on the map just through this competition," says Moe Levy. "These people didn't even know where Winnipeg was and suddenly all these international bigwigs in the world of architecture were coming here."

Sixty-three architects, several from as far away as Australia and India, indicated a serious expression of interest and provided initial renderings of how they envisioned the museum. In the end, thirty were invited to submit more detailed designs the following year. That total was then reduced to eight: three architects were

selected from the United States, two from Canada, and one each from Denmark, South Africa, and India. These semi-finalists received $12,000 each to further develop their designs.

The announcement of the eight semi-finalists on March 18, 2004, and the public display of their models for the CMHR at the Forks for the next ten days, captured the imagination of the city. It was "possibly the most important art show ever to open in the city," as David O'Brien of the *Winnipeg Free Press* put it that same day. "Unlike most art exhibitions, this one really matters and it won't leave people scratching their heads. It's all about our future and the image we'll project to the world." Or as Gail Asper, one of the members of the jury, said, "Even with our exceedingly high expectations, we were truly moved by the extraordinary sensitivity, vision, intellect, and transcendent qualities of the proposals. When people think of Canada, they'll think of this building."

right The three finalists in the international design competition for the CMHR with Moe Levy and Gail Asper. From L to R: Moe Levy, Gilles Saucier, Dan Hanganu, Antoine Predock, and Gail Asper.

facing The Architectural Review Committee comes together to select winning design for the CMHR. Back row from L to R: Róisín Heneghan, Jane Durante, Michael Bliss, Robert Fulford, J. Max Bond Jr., and Raymond Moriyama. Front row from L to R: Victor Rabinovitch, Gustavo Da Roza, Gail Asper, Moe Levy, and David M. Covo.

Indeed, if the goal of the museum's organizers was to electrify Winnipeggers and Canadians in general, they succeeded brilliantly. The eight singular designs—three of them were vividly described as "a glass tower that rises from a glass cloud," a "random plate structure that stretches out like a great jungle cat," and "skeletal totemic elements that transpierce the visual axis"—were, as a *Winnipeg Free Press* editorial added the following day, not the kind of buildings you find in Winnipeg.

Naturally, the hundreds of people who stopped by the Forks to examine the designs expressed their opinions. During the next week, the *Winnipeg Free Press* received hundreds of comments about the designs, as did the Asper Foundation office, which was bombarded with mail and telephone calls. And whether they approved of the semi-finalist selections or not, people were certainly talking about it. "Everyone wants to be an architect," said Gail Asper, "including me."

Six weeks later, the jury, working in top secret, whittled down the list to three finalists, that trio being awarded $100,000 each just for their trouble. The top contenders were Antoine Predock from New Mexico and two Montreal architectural firms—Saucier + Perrotte Architectes, and Dan Hanganu Architects and The Arcop Group. Another round of intense media commentary and scrutiny followed in which the three finalists' designs were dissected. The exhausting contest lasted eighteen months, until an international jury awarded the prize to Antoine Predock, whose proposed design, at $255,607,320, was slightly higher than his two competitors and $55 million higher than the competition directive that the museum should not exceed $200 million. "There was sticker shock with Predock's design," admits Moe Levy, "but the jury felt that it met all that we had asked the competitors to do."

Both Moe and Gail remember the competition and jury process as arduous but fun and

enlightening. At the outset of the competition process, Levy had consulted Winnipeg architect Morley Blankstein. He put Levy in touch with one of his former partners, R. Douglas Gillmor, who had worked for many years as the program director of the architectural program at the University of Calgary. Gillmor agreed to be one of nine members of the Technical Review Committee that would be responsible for ensuring the CMHR architectural design competition met professional standards. He later described his involvement in the project as "the most interesting two years of my life."

Gillmor had competed in other competitions as well as served on juries. However, he suggested that the competition for the CMHR and the jury that selected its design were unique because the CMHR is such a unique project: "It is not another city hall." Normally, an architectural jury has seven members, but the CMHR's jury had eleven members. "You needed a diverse group of individuals, men and women

from a variety of backgrounds," he adds. Hence, five of the eleven members of the jury, including Moe Levy and Gail Asper, the jury's chair, were non-architects.

In assembling the jury, or the Architectural Review Committee as it was called, Levy first contacted Róisín Heneghan, one of the founders of the Dublin-based firm Heneghan Peng Architects, winner of the 2003 competition to build the Grand Egyptian Museum in Cairo. She was helpful and agreed to serve as a juror for the CMHR. Other members of the Architectural Review Committee consisted of Toronto historian Michael Bliss; the New York–based African-American architect J. Max Bond Jr.; David M. Covo, an associate professor and past director of the School of Architecture at McGill University; Winnipeg architect Gustavo Da Roza; Vancouver architect Jane Durante; Toronto-based journalist Robert Fulford; Toronto architect Raymond Moriyama; and Victor Rabinovitch, from 2001 to 2011 the president and CEO of the Canadian

above, facing Antoine Predock's cloud encompasses more than five thousand square metres of windows and symbolizes the wings of a white dove, the symbol for peace, that envelops the building.

ANTOINE PREDOCK'S concept for the museum was inspired by Canadian landscapes—vast prairie skies, northern lights, and snow and ice—as well as by Canadian cultures, including indigenous cultures. The imagery of icebergs, tree roots, and outstretched wings influenced the form of the building.

The average floor-to-ceiling height of each level is 5.2 metres, creating a sense of vastness and openness within the museum. The immense glass cloud that encapsulates the building fills the upper portion of the museum with light, completing the visitor's journey from darkness to enlightenment.

The museum has four main sections: the cloud, the roots, the mountain, and the Tower of Hope.

The Cloud

The cloud, which encompasses more than five thousand square metres of windows, is meant to symbolize the wings of a white dove, the symbol for peace, embracing the building. The cloud is also an allusion to the vaporous state of water. The clouds in the sky reflect on the bluish windows, which look opaque from the exterior. The glass cloud, which also looks opaque from the exterior, provides a wonderful view of Winnipeg.

The Roots

Four large roots at the base of the museum ground the building to the land on which it sits. Once completed, three of the roots will be covered in prairie grasses. They will contain a diversity of services, including the museum's store, a restaurant, a temporary gallery, a theatre, and classrooms for school groups. The fourth root will be covered in Tyndall limestone steps, which can serve as an outdoor amphitheatre.

The Mountain

The mountain, made of Tyndall limestone from Manitoba that is more than 450 million years old, is a balance to the glass cloud. The heart of the museum, the mountain will hold the permanent exhibit spaces.

The Tower of Hope

At the end of your visit, if you are looking for a challenge, or a panoramic view of the city of Winnipeg, you can climb the spiral staircase or take the elevator up to the viewing platform located in the Tower of Hope.

SOURCE: *Courtesy of the Canadian Museum for Human Rights*

110

Museum of Civilization and Canadian War
Museum.

Details of the deliberations remain confidential, yet several members have indicated
they were intense. "It was an extremely high-powered experience, which I thought was characterized by constant discussion of the highest
standards," recalls Michael Bliss about his first
and only experience with an architectural jury.
At each stage of the process, the results were
made public, and so a variety of individuals
weighed in.

The final decision was not unanimous but
this was how Gail Asper summed up the verdict: "It wasn't that the jury necessarily all loved
Predock, but the terms of reference were that
the design had to be 'original, iconic, something
that had not been done before, and had an inspirational feel to it.' The jurors did all feel that
Predock's entry absolutely fit those criteria...
His design, literally and metaphysically rooted

to the site, rises out of it almost like a geological
formation." It was the New Mexico architect's
ability to focus on what another jury member
called "a strong sense of appropriateness combined with a careful interpretation of regional
identity" that won him the prize.

Michael Bliss concurs. "I particularly
remember that one of the reasons for our
enthusiasm about the Predock presentation
was that it presented an aesthetically optimistic framework for thinking about the human
rights experience," he says. "We were certainly
conscious of trying to fit the form of the
museum to our understanding of its mandate...
One of the appealing things to me about Predock's design was that it represented the sense of
aspiration towards freedom that we associate
with the western North American experience,
both Canadian and American."

The contest followed its rules so strictly that
one world-famous architect was eliminated
when his boards were filed ten minutes after
the deadline. The crunch moment for each
entry came when the finalists had to survive
a four-hour interview that touched on all of
the project's details. "I spent the six most
intensive months of my life building a big-scale model and getting prepared," Predock
recalled. Although he has gained a remarkable
international reputation for original work, he
ranked the Winnipeg assignment, which professionally qualified as North America's most

complex construction project, as the toughest and most demanding assignment of his career. One worry expressed at the time was Predock's unfamiliarity with Winnipeg's dramatic climate. Local architectural firms Smith Carter and Crosier Kilgour & Partners were charged with "transforming Predock's design into a reality for the public experience"—snowstorms included.

One untold story of the architectural contest involved a renowned architect. Even before the contest was launched, Moe Levy, who knows the value of everything that doesn't move, found himself in Los Angeles and phoned this individual to find out if he might be interested in submitting one of his unique designs for the museum. "It's going to cost you $3 million for me just to open a file," Levy was told, so the idea was abandoned.

112

top Architect Antoine Predock and Moe Levy of the Asper Foundation, April 26, 2006.

above The Architectural Review Committee enjoying a laugh during a break from the deliberations. Back row from L to R: Michael Bliss, Róisín Heneghan, Robert Fulford, J. Max Bond Jr., and David M. Covo. Front row from L to R: Gail Asper, Gustavo Da Roza, Moe Levy, Jane Durante, and Victor Rabinovitch. Missing: Raymond Moriyama.

facing A jubilant Antoine Predock and the Architectural Review Committee. From L to R: Raymond Moriyama, David M. Covo, Róisín Heneghan, Jane Durante, Babs Asper (deputy founder and co-chairman of the Asper Foundation), Michael Bliss, Moe Levy, Gail Asper, Robert Fulford, Antoine Predock, J. Max Bond Jr., and Victor Rabinovitch.

During the decision-making process, the issue came up as to whether the museum project ought to be reduced in its scope—specifically its cost, which was finally determined to be $351 million. In comparison, the new opera house was built in downtown Toronto for a relatively modest $180 million. Some partners, while supporting the idea of the CMHR, wanted to drastically reduce costs by placing less emphasis on the building and more on its contents. A Plan B design for the museum was developed that would have resembled a department store with an added tower and fancy front doors, reducing the cost to a mere $100 million.

Gail Asper quickly scotched that approach. She pleaded, "Let's remember what we're trying to do here. Look out at this Winnipeg landscape! What have we got? Grey square box after grey box and another grey square box! When you look out at Jerusalem, for example, what catches your eye? The Dome of the Rock. It's round. It's bright. It's different. It's beautiful. We just can't

have more of the same here." Her determination knew no bounds. When some of Predock's assistants reported that the original plans for coating some of the buildings' ramps and walls in alabaster would have to be abandoned because of that translucent material's high costs, Gail vetoed such a diversion from the original design and raised enough extra funds to cover the cost.

In many ways, Winnipeg remains a medieval fortress city, with invisible moats and social obstructions. But Antoine Predock managed to bridge the gap with his design. When his contest entry originally arrived in Winnipeg, before the voting started, Moe Levy put the boards of Predock's startling design where Gail would see them. "She looked, and looked again. Then ran back into her office," he recalls. Gail confirmed her instant emotional reaction and commented, "We don't cry very often in these offices... But when I saw Antoine's design I went upstairs and sobbed—I was that moved." The rest is history.

07

A NEW MEXICAN GRABS THE PRIZE

THE CANADIAN MUSEUM for Human Rights was never meant to be a depository for the rickety remnants of Aunt Lilly's souvenirs from her trackless hoarding expeditions. Instead, this is nothing less an authentically impressive call to action for human rights the world over. Encased in the most elaborate "skin" since the great pyramids of Egypt, the $351-million structure boasts a multitude of purposes, most of them being antidotes for demagoguery, platforms for justifications, and a virtual sea of red herrings. Included in its terms of reference but never mentioned is the intention to share a sprinkling of the glory showered on the prize-winning, wave-like roof that covers the Sydney Opera House in Australia that was universally recognized as a transformational phenomenon. The CMHR is the last best west bid by Winnipeg, the ambitious and worthy capital of Manitoba, to gain equal recognition for its similarly unique project. Gail Asper, who raised most of its private sector funds for its construction, firmly believes the museum

ought to be only the first step in her city's reincarnation. "When we finish with this, we must move on to something else," she maintains, "that proves once and for all to Winnipeggers that we don't need to perpetuate our downtrodden mentality—the idea that nothing good ever happens here. Let's move on to other projects."

Competition aside, the new museum is a glorious structure, meant to impress not only by what it is but also by the positive influence its staff and visitors are expected to yield. This is not another public service boondoggle or a political football. It is, for once, an altruistic and urgently required facility to improve the vital arena of how we treat one another. It will mean nothing if it doesn't make the people whose actions deserve it become furious and frantic when, following due process, they are forbidden to continue doing unto others what they don't want done to themselves. And that applies to anybody, anywhere, who is abusing human rights.

Meanwhile, the museum's architecture is bound to trigger lively debate. What did Antoine Predock, this baldly outspoken Yankee architect from New Mexico, have against straight lines? It isn't easy to find one that's more than twelve inches long in this impressive oddity of an original showcase. ("I don't like linear points," says he. "I like episodic, purposefully choreographed movement where you're continually exposed to different conditions of space and light.") The dozen galleries of exhibits, their walls clad in native limestone, are stacked like a rock face, parading in vertical cadence, exhibiting the evidence of human rights sagas gone wrong. Unlike most museums, which at worst may elicit boredom, this one goes to the root of things, raising vital issues from the day it opened. No plastic-boned dinosaurs haunt these galleries. Instead, it will be the witnesses and perpetrators of human rights abuses who will become the targeted troublemakers—their critics, the welcomed reformer.

Civil liberties are an issue like no other; everyone has a personal and intense obligation in these rights being honoured and expanded. Their outcomes rule our lives and decide our futures. The architects and planners never for a moment considered the Canadian Museum for Human Rights merely as a series of fancy exhibition halls. The history that will be replicated here will be the best and worst of human sagas through history, not just in Canada but the world. When individual rights conflict with collective liberties, it means trouble. But that, too, will be this museum's mandate. The planning and building of this vertical zoo of contradictory emotions was quarrelsome enough; its daily output of charges and counter-charges will be reminiscent of a championship tennis tournament, with witnesses of the verbal sparring turning their heads in unison from one source of praise or discord to the next. The museum's greatest value will be in focusing public opinion on the differences, and resolving them. If that sounds like no museum you've ever heard of, the answer is "precisely."

AT THE LEVEL of giving birth to this daring and emphatically one-off project, the museum is bound to bestow even more honours on Antoine Predock, its chief architect, and the resident savant of the entire shooting match. Widely recognized as one of architecture's most daring planners and executors, he is even more "one-off" than his building. His individual architectural style brings to his profession a wide swath of originality, as do his painfully honest comments. He once described himself as being "so obsessive about my work, I know I'm close to being clinically insane at times. I'm sure I am. But it's working for me."

His architecture is more art than science, an outgrowth of his considerations of how Mother Earth connects with humanity—and by extension, with the organic elements of his unusual designs. Debate and criticism doesn't rile this master architect—not one bit. It only encourages him. In assessing his work, Canadian visitors must never forget that Predock knew exactly what he intended doing: to build a museum that would be like no other, in that it would take its visitors' breaths away. He has achieved precisely that.

Predock in person? Just make sure you call him Antoine. "Yeah, well, look—my father's name was Tony," he privately explains, "and he called me Tony Junior. That didn't fit the circumstances, so I went back to my full first name, Antoine."

D'accord. Zut alors… You have created a miracle at the Forks—a beacon for human rights the world over. Rest easy, your secret is safe with us. Nobody named Tony Junior could have invented such a boffo silo with flashing lights, reaching for the stars.

Booted and spurred, the seventy-six-year-old miracle worker has done it all. We know how difficult this project turned out to be. One example: the museum's foundations sit on porous limestone that was punctured by underground rivers and caves, and sand dunes, with pesky clay and toxic methane formations. That was under the surface; on top, there was a small mountain of discarded fast-food wrappers, blowin' in the wind. "It was a miracle something could be built here," Predock admitted during construction. "It has been a challenge, but one that we were up for."

In March 1992, *Vanity Fair,* the American celebrity house organ, described him as "the outlaw of American architecture. Where others in his profession are cool, urbane and cerebral, he is physical and intuitive, a whirling force of nature." Born in the Ozarks of possible Québécois ancestry on his father's side, he has spent his adulthood deep in the heart of the New Mexican desert, popularized by the iconic American artist Georgia O'Keeffe.

Every Predock building fits neatly into its topography. His designs snuggle into the folds of nature's surfaces and are built less to appear distinctive than to look compatible in their settings. Even the prevailing climate, wind direction, and sun patterns are taken into account. He approaches architecture as an

117

118

abstract landscape series of art objects that he tweaks into unexpectedly intriguing patterns. "Before you get down seriously to designing," he insists, "you have to experience the site with your body." Similarly, to enter his new museum, visitors must find their way through four gigantic stone arms extending out from the centre of the building, calibrated to block northern and northwestern winds, and descend below ground level into Mother Earth, where everyone's journey begins. This connection is a dramatic curtain raiser for a riveting climb that climaxes, many impressions later, in the Tower of Hope. The building's gossamer-covered structure is twelve storeys high, while the tower rises an extra eleven floors, with a glassed-in viewing platform. It was Gail Dexter Lord, arguably Canada's foremost museum expert, who was very much involved in the early plan and insisted on the essential presence of a distinctive tower. It has the aura of a luxurious lighthouse, a beacon to celebrate Canada's respect for diversity, inclusiveness, and personal responsibility. Its peak will top one hundred metres and sit on the tower's glass "cloud," suggestive of doves' wings, wrapped protectively over one another.

The mood that Predock's design exudes is improvisational of the highest calibre, reminiscent of a Miles Davis jazz solo—made up on the spot but containing predetermined rhythms and harmonics that give it *gravitas* delivered with a beat. Like the emotionally driven trumpet player, the architect integrates body and

soul in his designs. "There is a realm of translation from research to the project that you can't explain how it happens—it's kind of supernatural," Predock admits. "You want to leave it alone and not try to rationalize, but it has an aura of magic and alchemy." In April 1988, *Time* magazine's art critic Kurt Andersen was right on the button when he wrote: "Predock is creating a remarkable body of work—tough and sensual, fabulously imagined, altogether persuasive."

PREDOCK'S CV OCCUPIES forty-eight single-spaced pages. The numbers alone tell the story: he has won eighty-four awards for his architectural projects, including the prestigious American Institute of Architects Gold Medal; exhibited pages out of his sketchbooks at numerous art galleries, notably the Venice Biennale in 1996; taught at fourteen universities, including a stint at the Harvard Graduate School of Design in 1987; and won several valuable travelling fellowships, headed by the coveted Rome Prize in 1985. He has also written seven books and contributes to a dozen online venues.

"Architecture is a ride," he maintains. "The idea of a motorcycle in the landscape confirms a kind of closure for me, a technological, experiential closure." The collection of a baker's dozen of motorcycles that occupy the studio is his second passion. It features a British-built 1951 Vincent Black Shadow. That weird-looking contraption is arguably the most radically designed

racing machine. Instead of being built around a frame, it uses the engine as its main support system. You can do repairs by taking off parts that turn into tools; flip a wheel over to change the gear ratio. It is one of the fastest production motorcycles ever built, having been clocked at 159 miles per hour, though to achieve that speed its daredevil driver had to lie straight across the seat, legs pointing backwards, dressed only in a bathing suit to reduce the wind drag.

HIS STUDIOS WHERE everything happens are in the Old Town quarter of Albuquerque, where Predock employs a dozen architects (under the supervision of his main assistants) plus support staffs. Explaining how he tailored the museum's structure to serve its global reach, he admits it was a tall order. "Predock was born to build the Museum for Human Rights," wrote critic Robbie Moore in an architectural magazine. That rings true. His studio is a huddle of huts and workstations, second-generation

helpers, and ongoing projects. The working areas resemble the jumble of a movie set. But he makes it sound as if he was aware of the breadth of his mandate, so that the museum would resonate with the appropriate echoes. Parts of the finished edifice feel more like a cathedral than a museum.

It was Martin Heidegger, arguably the greatest of the German philosophers, who explained that the significance of our dwellings on earth must be understood in relation to "the primal oneness of earth and sky"—earth as "the serving bearer, blossoming and rising up into plant and animal"; sky as "the vaulting path of the sun, the course of the changing moon, the wandering glitter of the stars ..." Attempting to define architecture in terms of its connections with the universe at large is a pitch not likely to be used by your average real estate agent, but it goes to the heart of this unusual architect's operational code. Apart from the master's degree he earned at

New York's Columbia University, his education shied away from architecture as such, and specialized in almost everything else. He crossed Europe from Paris to Istanbul by motorcycle, studying various cultures; he studied painting and drawing in parallel with his architectural studies, and co-directed a dance company along with Metropolitan Opera dancer—later choreographer—Jennifer Masley, who became his first wife and muse. Antoine and his current wife, the sculptor Constance DeJong, have been together twenty-five years. Their work shares geometric similarities, but what he finds most inspirational in her sculpture and drawings is a sense of a deeper content that doesn't depend on literal representation. Antoine reflects, "I think of real architecture as an adventure, extremely physical but mostly informed by spirit. I would place architecture more here [pointing to his heart] than here [indicating his head]—that place one points to when one thinks of his or her inner place that operates independently of intellectual processes."

BACK IN NEW MEXICO during the 1960s, he kept a horse in the Old Town, fulfilling his brief cowboy fantasy, "until the manure pile got so high that the city busted me."

He used the occasion of our meeting to restate his thesis. "Architecture has an aura that one cannot invoke in one's work. It is either there or it isn't—like the idea of *duende* in a flamenco performance, which means a manifestation of spirit in a performance that renders the music and dance timeless."

His projects are known for being site-specific, which sets up tensions between the workshops where they are conceived and the widely varied locations where they are built and utilized. As a human rights museum, the CMHR had to be designed with a global reach, keeping in mind that its contents must resonate with cultures that often have little in common except discord and suspicion.

Antoine is as unpredictable as a lone wolf howling at a purple moon, situated at the head of his pack, but always looking behind him, ready to leap either way. Both hated and loved, he is mostly envied. Those whose psyches he touches feel every emotion except neutrality. Money-minded he certainly is, but there is a part of him nobody can buy. In an occupation that demands pleasing clients with peculiar assignments, he retains his own pride and prejudices. Whatever happens to this remarkable artist who gave us his most evocative architectural creation, he knows that, as always, he can depend on the twin sources of his character that will never let him down: the ability to make his own luck, and the determination of a canal horse.

121

08

BUILDING THE MUSEUM

THE FIRST TIME Todd Craigen of PCL Construction opened the set of blueprints for the Canadian Museum for Human Rights, in January 2007, he was stunned. "We started looking and flipping through pages and pages, and I remember looking around the table and asking, 'Holy cow, is this even possible?' At the end of the day, we put a lot of time and effort into answering that question."

Craigen studied architectural engineering at the Saskatchewan Institute of Applied Science and Technology and has close to twenty years' experience in the construction business. He relocated with his family from Ottawa to Winnipeg to take charge of the museum project. With military precision, he diligently prepared his army of workers for one of the biggest jobs of their careers: the building of the CMHR—with an interior measuring twenty-four thousand square metres and twelve storeys high. The new Winnipeg football stadium may have been a larger undertaking, but at $351 million

(compared with $190 million for the stadium), no construction project in the history of the city was as expensive or as elaborate as making Antoine Predock's unique design a reality.

It was, Craigen says, "one of the most complicated and sophisticated construction projects . . . undertaken in North America. One look at the iconic architecture and you can get a sense for the complexities in the geometry and shape of the building. Taking those free-form curved surfaces into constructible shapes is an enormous technical challenge, to be able to warp or mould constructible materials into these complex geometries . . . In some cases, we had to alter the way that things were designed and make them more economical and constructible."

Over a more than three-year period starting in April 2009, Craigen was responsible for the thousands of builders, electricians, structural engineers, mechanical engineers, landscape architects, and sustainability consultants, as

well as machinery of every size and type, that were employed. Each day, at least 350 workers descended on the Forks site to erect what skeptics had said was an impossible feat. Steel beams and supports had to be brought in from as far away as Belgium, and nearly seventeen hundred specially made panes of glass, strong enough to withstand the bitterly cold temperatures of Winnipeg in January and the heat of the summers, were shipped in from Germany.

Craigen compared the assignment to a relay race. "Whoever has the first baton has the critical path. That was us," he explained in an October 2010 interview with the *Winnipeg Free Press*. "We do the foundation and the concrete. And we're racing as fast as we can to hand off

the baton to Walters, the structural steel people [from Hamilton, Ontario]. They will go hard for six to eight months and then they hand it off to [Gartner Steel and Glass] to install all the glazing. And if all goes well, we'll be able to finish up, hand over the keys to the Chevy, and we're out of there. At least, that's the plan."

By the time he was finished, Craigen was so committed to the project that he became an active CMHR fundraiser and oversaw PCL's matching of donations up to $250,000 in 2011. "I've never before taken up the cause for one of our clients," he says, "but for this I went out on tour with Gail and Moe. This project is one of those unique once-in-a-lifetime opportunities to work on a building that is truly remarkable

and a project that is truly remarkable. The building, the architecture, and the construction is one thing and that legacy will live on as people visit the building. But the message and mission of the building itself resonated with everyone involved in the project. We were part of something that has a real chance to make a difference."

More than a year before Craigen assumed command, the museum had funded a $550,000 archaeological dig, the largest ever completed at the Forks, in compliance with provincial laws and with respect for the history of the site. The team of archaeologists working at the dig discovered a two-hundred-square-metre space

with pottery shards and a human footprint believed to have been eight hundred years old.

As soon as the frozen Winnipeg tundra had thawed, PCL construction crews began the arduous process of digging the holes for the 370 concrete piles and 148 caissons, some dug down as deep as twenty-five metres into the Manitoba bedrock. These secured the museum's massive structure, but enormous problems with the caissons delayed construction and increased the costs. As PCL hit about seventeen metres below existing grade, the caisson contractor encountered a veritable underground jungle: clay, fractured rock, and caverns, some as big as a compact car. Then there was the high water flow

and high levels of methane gas at or above the seventeen-metre mark. As Craigen explains, "In the caisson holes that had high water flows, the caisson had itself required that a steel sleeve be installed to protect uncured concrete from being eroded away by water and, as a result, in a large number of these circumstances, the steel sleeve had to be abandoned and left in the caisson hole."

Needless to say, these difficulties were worrisome. Because of the subsurface rock conditions, this work took a total of ten months to complete, increased the budget by a total of $8 million, and set the overall project schedule back by three months. "The CMHR caisson foundation ended up to be a sore point for everyone involved," adds Craigen. "There were countless late-night meetings and presentations to CMHR executives and board members to explain how this happened and what could be done to remedy the situation. The entire team held out hope that eventually the caisson situation would improve as we moved out of certain areas of the building; however, the issues persisted and in some cases got worse each month, as the poor subsurface rock conditions were ubiquitous up until the day the last caisson was drilled."

On hand to supervise all of this were Aboriginal elders. Museum officials had asked them to be present so that the sacred Forks land could be properly blessed. And so, into each deep crevice, workmen gingerly placed the medicine bags of sage, sweetgrass, tobacco, and

facing, above Nearly seventeen hundred specially made panes of glass, strong enough to withstand the bitterly cold temperatures of Winnipeg in January and the heat of the summers, were shipped in from Germany.

cedar the elders provided. The medicine bags had been handcrafted by a group of elders from Thunderbird House, an Aboriginal cultural and spiritual centre in Winnipeg. The elders had originally requested that one of their representatives from Thunderbird House be present to place the medicine bags in each hole; however, logistically and from a health and safety perspective, that was simply not possible. As it turned out, one of the PCL workers from the foundation crew was Aboriginal and closely followed traditional teachings. Once Craigen presented this individual's credentials to the elders, they were more than satisfied that the worker would be able to complete this task with the necessary care and respect. This symbolic ceremony was the way to ask for Mother Earth's forgiveness for the digging and for the Canadian Museum for Human Rights to be brought into the world showing the respect the museum itself hoped to engender.

top Stantec Consulting archaeologist Nicole Skalesky excavates a bison skull found upside down at the Forks site, 2009.

above Quaternary archaeologists Sid Kroker and Ernie Reichert show a cast of the eight-hundred-year-old human footprint discovered at the CMHR dig.

facing A Stantec Consulting crew conducts archaeological monitoring around a few of the 148 caissons and piles at the museum's base.

above Quaternary archaeologists conduct block excavations under a screened tent at the CMHR dig site in June 2008.

facing Quaternary archaeologists conduct excavations at the CMHR dig site in early July 2008.

OVER 400,000 ARTIFACTS dating as far back as AD 1100 were recovered from the CMHR digs, conducted in two stages between 2008 and 2012 by Quaternary Consultants, led by senior archaeologist Sid Kroker, and by Stantec Consulting, led by senior archaeologist David McLeod. The first stage was the largest block archaeological excavation ever conducted in Manitoba.

Among the significant findings were:

▶ A large number of hearths (191) in the relatively small excavation area, possibly the highest concentration of any site in Canada. This suggests long-term seasonal habitation, raising questions about interpretation of the role of the Forks as simply a stopping and trading place.

▶ At least five completely new and previously unseen types of ceramic pottery, which seem to represent a period of rapid cultural change that took place over two to three hundred years, between AD 1100 and 1400. This suggests that different groups from a wide geographic area met here to interact, trade, form alliances, and marry—resulting in the evolution of a "homegrown" localized pottery type distinct from those of Saskatchewan or North Dakota. The pottery findings may also refute the theory that Anishinaabe (Ojibwa) people did not move into the Forks until the fur-trade era, and instead suggest they had been using the site for hundreds of years previously, along with many other groups.

▶ The presence of maize and bean residues on ceramics, scapula hoe fragments, and squash knives, supporting theories that farming took place along the Red River, particularly since evidence was also found at a dig at Lockport.

▶ An intact ceremonial pipe adorned with a beaver effigy (the bowl being the nose), similar to those made by Aboriginal peoples far to the south, evidence that sophisticated long-distance trade networks existed.

▶ A high concentration of sacred materials such as ceremonial pipe fragments, possible sucking tubes, and a significant presence of red ochre, supporting theories that the site was a place of peaceful meeting, alliance building, and celebration.

▶ There was no evidence that the CMHR site has ever been a burial ground.

SOURCE: *Courtesy of the Canadian Museum for Human Rights*

PCL poured more than 18,000 cubic metres of concrete, partly to create the museum's mammoth foundation, weighing in at 35,000 tonnes, "about the weight of 3,000 fully grown male elephants," according to *Winnipeg Free Press* reporter Geoff Kirbyson. The steel used in the construction, Kirbyson also noted, exceeded 5,400 tonnes, "equal to that in 27 diesel-electric locomotives." Erecting the steel beams took ten months of manpower, and the installation required an acute professionalism to ensure each one fit precisely as measured.

Creating Predock's Alabaster Labyrinth, or "wedge canyon," as the construction team referred to it, with its series of ramps, was one

of the more challenging tasks. Architects from the Winnipeg firm Smith Carter were asked to figure out the best way to maintain Predock's original design while complying with the city's building code and ensuring the museum would not crumble in the process. "Every time we moved something to meet code, the engineers would tell us, 'That's great, but the wall is going to fall down,'" Jim Weselake, a senior partner at Smith Carter, told the *Winnipeg Free Press.* "So we went back to the drawing board and looked for another solution."

The glass panes, the museum's most distinguishing feature, were yet another challenge, one ultimately solved by Stefan Zimmermann,

the director of operations of Gartner Steel and Glass in Würzburg, Germany. Once he learned more about the museum, Zimmermann was astounded by Winnipeg's extreme temperatures but felt certain that his firm, celebrated for its complex glass structures, could create the necessary product—including Predock's twenty-three-storey Tower of Hope and glass cloud that wraps around the museum like a mother holding a newborn child.

"Besides the detailed design, fabrication, and installation of the cloud and Tower of Hope facades, we were engaged by means of a design-assist process to convert the design intent of the architect into a workable solution for the building envelope," he says. "This solution had to consider the expectations of the owner and the designers from a visual point of view, the required performance criteria for the building envelope, and the budget requirements. To achieve these goals, extensive geometrical studies had to be carried out in combination with exploring different typologies for the secondary structure and the glazing of the envelope. The most intricate portion of the job was this first intense design-assist phase, which was a tightrope walk between aesthetics, engineering, and budget. Looking on the completed project now, we are extremely proud to have been responsible for creating the building envelope as part of it."

134

The last pane of glass—tested like all the rest in the Winnipeg company E.H. Price's cold-weather chamber—was installed near the end of September 2012. The glass from Germany was only one component of the international character of the museum. The stone used in the museum's construction came from Tyndall, Manitoba, as well as from Mongolia. A portion of the steel was imported from Turkey, and the alabaster for the winding ramps connecting the exhibits and part of Predock's original design were shipped in from northern Spain, near Barcelona. The alabaster ramps—created from white-speckled rectangle blocks pieced together—are magnificent, and give the museum a European flavour. Few buildings in Canada, let alone Winnipeg, have such a distinguishing feature.

CALL IT THE wow factor. The objective of museum officials was to ensure that every person walking into the building would be wowed.

That, at any rate, is one of the stated goals of Stuart Murray, who was appointed the CMHR's inaugural CEO in September 2009. This also explains Murray's support for the alabaster ramps, though he does not hesitate to credit Gail for their inclusion.

Murray was an excellent choice for the position. His career had been a mixture of business, politics, and management—with rock 'n' roll thrown in for good measure. He is a diehard Prairie boy. Murray was born in 1954 in the tiny village of Lestock in central Saskatchewan and grew up twenty-five kilometres east, in the next "big" stop on the CPR's main line, Punnichy. His mother, Jean, was a town councillor. Murray relocated to Winnipeg to attend the University of Manitoba and then moved on to Toronto to complete his studies in agricultural science at what was then the Ryerson Polytechnical Institute. There, he lucked into a job as the road manager for Blood, Sweat & Tears, the popular rock-jazz band then featuring singer David

Clayton-Thomas. In 1982, his eclectic career path took him to the Canadian Opera Company as its media director, and then to Ottawa in 1985 and a gig as Prime Minister Brian Mulroney's tour director and advance man. Those connections cemented his ties to the Progressive Conservative Party.

In the meantime, Murray had married Ashleigh Everett, the daughter of Winnipeg businessman Douglas Everett, the owner of the Domo Gasoline Corporation, who had been appointed to the Senate in 1966 by Lester Pearson. In 1989, Murray became Domo's vice-president and four years later replaced his father-in-law as CEO of the company. In this new position, he also emerged as a key Manitoba organizer for the Conservative Party and gained a high profile in Winnipeg. Following the provincial election in 1999, which saw the NDP and Gary Doer defeat the Progressive Conservatives (PCs), its long-time leader Gary Filmon decided to step down. Murray, "affable and understated," as the *Winnipeg Free Press* aptly described him, was the popular choice of the party's officials and won the leadership by acclamation in November 2000.

Gary Doer, who grabbed the middle of the political spectrum and gave Manitobans solid government, was a tough opponent to beat. In the 2003 provincial election, although Murray

138

ran a good campaign and proposed removing taxing powers from local school boards, Doer and the NDP easily won another term in office. After that, there was grumbling in the party about Murray. He received an endorsement at the PC annual meeting held in Brandon in 2004, but within a year a small cadre of MLAs were calling for a leadership review. At the next annual meeting, in November 2005, Murray received a vote of confidence from 55 per cent of the delegates; deciding that was insufficient, he stepped down as leader. After he resigned his seat as an MLA in September 2006, he was named the new president and CEO for the St-Boniface Hospital Research Foundation, a position he held until his appointment as head of the CMHR.

Murray says he was happy at the hospital, but when he received a call from the PMO inquiring if he was interested in becoming the museum's first CEO, it was an offer he could not refuse. His friends asked him if he realized the true extent of the challenges he would be facing, and he admits that his job "is like a series of landmines. Some you see and can maybe avoid; some you don't, you step on, and you've got to deal with." Indeed, within a week of his appointment, the fact that he, as provincial Tory leader, had voted against the NDP's decision to extend adoption and other familiar rights to gays and lesbians, became an issue in the media. Murray immediately reached out to the gay and lesbian community in Winnipeg and reassured them that they would "have a voice at the table"

and that "sexual orientation will be a theme explored at the museum." He added that as a political leader he was following the wishes of his caucus. "My personal belief," he asserted, "is dignity for all people."

As financial concerns swirled around the museum, Murray also had to deal with a number of high-profile staff departures. Patrick O'Reilly, who had been appointed the museum's chief operating officer in 2008, resigned. This was followed by the departures of Victoria Dickenson, the chief knowledge officer, who left Winnipeg for a job as head of the McMichael Canadian Art Collection in Kleinburg, Ontario, and soon after by Judith Dueck, the director of research, content, and scholarship, who retired. In the summer of 2013, Gail Stephens, the former chief administrative officer of the City of Winnipeg and since 2009 the city manager of Victoria, B.C., was appointed the CMHR's new chief operating officer. Susanne Robertson, a chartered accountant who had been recruited by the Friends in 2007, was appointed the museum's chief financial officer in September 2008. She worked closely with the CMHR's Board of Trustees and the federal government to ensure the project moved forward.

Naturally, the comings and goings at the CMHR was good news copy in Winnipeg and elsewhere, but much of it, Murray states, was based on misinformation. In all, between 2009 and 2012, twenty-four staff members left the museum, a few, Murray concedes, because of differences of opinion over what the content in

the museum should be, or because of concern about perceived federal government directives to tell more positive Canadian stories in the exhibits. "I have learned one thing," Murray says. "People are not blasé about the subject of human rights. Their passion is palpable and so sometimes it is narrow in focus and sometimes broader. But that's why you have a board with representative from across Canada."

In the fall of 2012, the museum lost its director of finance, director of facilities, and manager of sales and marketing. Stories in the press catalogued the alleged employee dissatisfaction, yet they were also highly exaggerated. Murray points out that in the cases of the director of finance and director of facilities, for example, both individuals left to pursue career advancements. Simply put, neither the federal Department of Canadian Heritage, nor

the museum board for that matter, has ever told the staff not to include one human rights story or another. The board, however, does have the obligation and responsibility for the overall theme of the museum, and celebrating Canadian content, including profiling Canadian human rights leaders, had always been part of the original plan. As in any start-up company, people gripe, and some *Winnipeg Free Press* columnists were only too happy to give weight to those complaints.

Murray took it all in stride, telling anyone who asked him that he felt both honoured and lucky to be associated with the museum. In response to several *Free Press* stories in December 2012 about the apparent difficulty of the CMHR in retaining its employees, Murray wrote in a letter to the newspaper, "Over the past four years, a remarkable group of women and

140

men have contributed to this project. But, yes, there were changes. Some people left, some were replaced and some positions changed or were eliminated, reflecting the evolution of our needs . . . [If] our turnover rate is deemed high, it is partly due to the challenging nature of our work, subject matter and public expectations. But it is not correct to suggest that the issue boils down to academics' ideas on museum content conflicting with that of museum-goers. Rather, in our discussions with your reporter about the various reasons for staff departures, we were trying to acknowledge that some staff—including (but not limited to) our researchers—might have felt frustrated if their personal commitments in approach or ideology did not fully align with the museum's inaugural exhibition plans."

These and other stories were all part of the media microscope the museum was placed under from the day it was announced. More pleasant for Murray was having the opportunity to meet the Queen.

On July 3, 2010, an oppressively hot summer day, Queen Elizabeth and Prince Philip visited Winnipeg for a mere six hours as part of their nine-day royal tour of Canada. The highlight of their brief stop in the city was to dedicate the cornerstone of the museum. For the occasion, the Queen had brought with her a stone she chose personally from the fields of Runnymede, England, close to the site where the Magna Carta was signed in 1215. Accompanied

by Stephen Harper, Premier Greg Selinger, and other Manitoba and federal politicians, Murray was introduced to the Queen, as was Gail Asper, outfitted in a wide-brimmed hat, and Moe Levy.

"May this museum serve as a beacon of peace and hope for all the people in the world," Her Majesty declared in the ceremony. In her speech, she called the museum "a symbol of the importance which Canada attaches to human rights . . . Here at the Forks, the symbolism of Magna Carta is now joined to the historical importance of this site, where Aboriginal peoples gathered for thousands of years to exchange views and resolve conflicts."

For Murray, it was another perfect day as CEO of the museum. And there would be more. In the months that followed, he signed a memorandum of understanding with the Embassy of the Netherlands to facilitate the promotion of human rights through joint projects and educational exchanges. Similar agreements were also soon signed with the University of Winnipeg and the University of Manitoba to advance human rights research and education. And, in December 2012, another memorandum of understanding was signed with the Canadian Teachers' Federation, the Assembly of First Nations, the Inuit Tapiriit Kanatami, and the Robert F. Kennedy Center for Justice and Human Rights to create a tool kit that teachers across Canada can use in the classroom to teach human rights in a consistent manner.

BEYOND DEALING WITH finances—which included the task of not only seeking additional government funding but also defending the value of the museum from detractors who argued that it was a waste of public money—and establishing links with other institutions, the other key issue that occupied Murray as soon as he moved into his makeshift office in the Government of Canada Victory Building on Main Street was the matter of the museum's content. The Ukrainian community's disapproval with the perceived slight to the Holodomor continued unabated. The unfortunate by-product of this dispute was the controversy it produced over the positioning of the Holocaust. Here was one of the worst human rights abuses in recorded history, in which an entire society's official personnel and resources were harnessed for the destruction of millions of Jews because they were of a different religion and culture. There was no denying the systematic nature of the Holocaust or the fact that there was at least an indirect connection between the Holocaust and the Universal Declaration of Human Rights (UDHR) adopted by the United Nations General Assembly in 1948. British historian Mark Mazower has argued, "The Holocaust … was much less central to perceptions in 1945 of what the war had been about than it is today," though the record of the atrocities surely must have weighed on the framers of the UDHR.

Nevertheless, other scholars offered their learned opinions, and informative and passionate letters to the editors were sent. In July 2012, Murray signed a memorandum of understanding with the National Memorial in Commemoration of Famines' Victims in Kiev. Some months later, this led to a visit to Canada by two Ukrainian scholars, Stanislav Kulchytsky, deputy director of the Institute of History of Ukraine at the National Academy of Sciences of Ukraine, and Lesya Onyshko, first deputy of the general director of the National Memorial in Commemoration of Famines' Victims in Ukraine, who gave lectures about their research on the Holodomor in Winnipeg, Edmonton, and Toronto.

Still the critics could not be appeased. "For three years now, the Ukrainian Canadian Congress has called publicly for an inclusive and equitable museum that would include both Holocaust and Holodomor galleries," Taras

Zalusky of the congress wrote in a letter to the *Winnipeg Free Press* on September 26, 2012. "To be perfectly clear, we do not oppose a Holocaust gallery in the museum. Because of its distinct pedagogical value to human-rights education, we have asserted that the Holodomor, arguably one of the greatest acts of genocide in 20th-century European history, should be displayed in a permanent and prominent gallery. The Ukrainian community's position has been consistent for the past decade and was in fact endorsed by the late Izzy Asper at a meeting and confirmed in a follow-up letter from the Asper Foundation in April 2003 in which he agreed to include the Holodomor."

From Murray's perspective, however, the museum was never intended to be a monument for every human rights tragedy ever perpetuated. "We're not here to memorialize past events," he said in a May 2011 interview. "This is about education through a human rights lens."

Several months earlier, after yet another public discussion of whose "rights" the museum would feature, he also had responded with a letter of his own to the *Winnipeg Free Press.* "Human rights issues are not simple; they are complex, thorny and often interconnected," wrote Murray. "Izzy Asper knew this when he dreamed up the Canadian Museum for Human Rights. Gail Asper knew this when she took over from Izzy. And the CMHR staff knows this well, as they are challenged daily to develop the CMHR's inaugural exhibits. Two years away from opening, controversy over the content of the exhibits already exists, and it is likely to continue until opening and beyond ... I would like to assure Canadians that the content of the museum will be inclusive, it will be diverse and it will be inspiring. Yes, indigenous rights and the Holocaust will be examined. So will many other issues: mass atrocities, gender issues, the rights of persons with disabilities, sexual orientation, children's rights, women's equality, labour rights, poverty, racism, language rights, age, migration-immigration, and others. The CMHR will explore past successes like the adoption of the Universal Declaration of Human Rights and current human rights abuses like the situation in Darfur. Most of all, the CMHR will inspire debate and dialogue among people about human rights issues and will encourage people to take a stand for human rights." By this point, the controversial debate about what would be displayed in the museum and how it would be presented was more than eight years old.

LAWYER AND human rights advocate Yude Henteleff, the chairman of the Content Advisory Committee (CAC)—which in 2007 became a sub-committee of the Board of Trustees of the CMHR—grew up on his family farm in St. Vital in the southeast part of Winnipeg during the 1930s. He attended École St. Germain and was the only Jewish student in the school. Small as a youngster, he was regularly chased and beaten by anti-Semitic bullies, until he fought them back with a stick. He also recalls walking down the street with his father: "A francophone kid

would approach us and say to my father, 'Bonjour, Juif,'—'Hello, Jew,'—as if it was nothing."

A kind and sensitive individual and a brilliant legal scholar, Henteleff never forgot these hateful incidents, which shaped his law career and passion for promoting human rights. Following Izzy's death, Moe Levy, in his role as executive director of the Friends, recruited Henteleff to chair the first content committee in 2005; little did Henteleff know that this job would occupy him for the next five years.

Henteleff understood it was the content that "lies at the heart of the museum," as the CAC final report of May 2010 outlined. Content development, though complex, was "the foundation and the framework upon which the whole meaning-making, storytelling experience is based. It produces the broad ideas and detailed examples that are given to the exhibition designer to turn into something magical."

A team of five scholars and specialists were assembled in 2005, and then another seven experts were added the following year. Besides Henteleff, the other CAC members who remained for the duration and participated in the cross-Canada public meetings in 2009–10 convened after the federal government assumed control of the project were Constance Backhouse, a law professor from the University of Ottawa and Henteleff's vice-chair; David Matas, a well-known Winnipeg human rights and immigration lawyer; Ken Norman, a law professor at the University of Saskatchewan and former head of the Saskatchewan Human

143

Rights Commission; Laurie Beachell, the national director of the Council of Canadians with Disabilities; Mary Eberts, a Toronto lawyer, author, and lecturer on issues of women's equality, Aboriginal rights, human rights, and the Charter of Rights and Freedoms; Diana Majury, an associate professor in the Department of Law at Carleton University; Patricia Monture, a Mohawk from Six Nations Grand River and a professor in the Department of Sociology at the University of Saskatchewan (who died in December 2010); and Steve Prystupa, a museum curator who has served as the curator of history and multicultural studies at the Manitoba Museum, as a prairie and northern historian with the Canadian Museum of Civilization, and as a museum funding consultant with the Department of Canadian Heritage. Other members of the first CAC were Ruth Selwyn, then the executive director of Equitas, the International Centre for Human Rights Education, and Anthony Hall, a professor of Globalization Studies at the University of Lethbridge, Alberta.

This group held a series of meetings with Ralph Appelbaum and his associates, who had been hired by the Friends in early 2004, and began the arduous process of trying to answer the tough questions. It involved, recalls Henteleff, "everything you could think of. What are human rights? What are the particulars about the evolution in Canada? To what extent was that evolution affected by events elsewhere? What uniqueness was there that was unique to us as a country in terms of our own evolution?

And that, of course, involved a full variety of vested interests."

Central to these early discussions were also the lessons to be learned from the Holocaust and how indifference has resulted in compliance with acts of genocide. "We already had established that in our own heads as a principle," continues Henteleff, "and so the mandate that we set for ourselves was to create and operate a new national museum in Winnipeg as a non-profit public corporation dedicated to presenting a comprehensive program of research and education." Even at that early stage, he says, the committee was in agreement that the museum's galleries should focus on Aboriginal issues, the Holocaust, the intolerance of Canadian society over the years, and the development of human rights in the country and internationally, with an emphasis on the United Nations Universal Declaration of Human Rights. An initial report was sent to Appelbaum in the spring of 2007 outlining these ideas and concepts. And then nothing happened.

Henteleff and his committee were ready to begin discussions with interested Canadians about the museum, but they were stymied by the political and financial negotiations over the museum. After the federal government took over the project in 2008, Patrick O'Reilly, who was installed as the chief operating officer (and acting CEO until September 2009), told Henteleff that in terms of the museum's content, "nothing is decided." The government wanted to reconsider everything about the museum's plan,

though in the end federal officials accepted Appelbaum's master plan and Henteleff's proposal (at a cost of $185,000) for a cross-country tour to speak to as many Canadians as possible about human rights and the CMHR.

The CAC under Henteleff's guidance was reconstituted and revamped. Backhouse, Beachell, Eberts, Majury, Matas, Monture, Norman, and Prystupa stayed on. They were joined by Natasha Bakht, an assistant professor at the University of Ottawa's Faculty of Law; Jaime Battiste from Eskasoni First Nation and a graduate of Dalhousie Law School; Jennifer Breakspear, a human rights activist; Derek Evans, the former deputy secretary general of Amnesty International; Sylvia Hamilton, an award-winning Nova Scotia filmmaker and writer; Guy Marchand of Parks Canada; Montreal lawyer Julie Latour; and Barbara Myers, the director of Business Development for Number TEN Architectural Group.

The CAC set an objective to hold open and honest public forums. From May 2009 to February 2010, CAC groups visited nine cities across Canada, from St. John's to Vancouver and as far north as Yellowknife and Whitehorse. Thousands of people showed up, many more than the CAC had anticipated. In Saskatoon, the meeting ran from seven o'clock in the morning until ten at night, and still not everyone who was there got an opportunity to make a presentation. The members of the CAC heard everything and anything; each person and group had a story to tell, whether it was about the Aboriginal experience at a residential school, a recent refugee claim, or the discrimination faced by LBGTQ community and disabled peoples. It was clear from these meetings that history and memory have an impact on individuals in many different ways as stories are shared with the next generations.

Of all the topics that were discussed, none resonated as much as the story of Canada's Aboriginals. There was a consensus from both indigenous and non-indigenous participants that the "gravity and significance" of the Aboriginal story must be emphasized and told to the fullest extent possible at the museum.

For Yude Henteleff, the many sessions he attended were eye-opening and educational.

Ken Norman has similar recollections. "At the roundtables was where the surprises came, because we had people who hadn't come with a prepared position," he says. "They just showed up and they sat around, and each of us served as a facilitator of about eight to ten folks around a table, all in one big conference room or ballroom of a hotel. We went for a couple of hours, and what surprised me was the remarkable cross-cultural dialogue that emerged … People were often just telling their own story and others were listening attentively and were making the connection with their own personal experiences."

The CAC's final report of May 25, 2010 (released four months later), written with input from all of its members, contained forty-eight recommendations on how to balance museology with human rights—no easy task. Among other suggestions, the CAC proposed that the museum continue to engage Canadians and experts on the development of its content.

After the CAC had concluded its work, Stuart Murray decided that he required a similar group of experts and scholars to personally advise him as CEO of the CMHR on human rights issues. He created the Human Rights Advisory Council (HRAC), of which he was the chair. Several of the former CAC members, including Yude Henteleff, Mary Eberts, and Ken Norman, were named to this new committee.

Yet, like anything to do with the museum's content, there were differences of opinion. "There's usually not agreement around the table,"

says Murray of his meetings with the council. He considers and weighs the advice he receives and then makes a decision. Mary Eberts did not agree with this process and quickly lost patience with the council's lack of influence. In July 2010 she resigned from the HRAC to protest what she argued was inaction on the part of Murray and museum officials, stating in a letter (later released to the media) that council did not have "any real opportunity to be of influence in the decision-making about the content and form of exhibits." Murray regretted her departure but disagreed with her assessment of what had transpired.

Two weeks before the CAC report was completed, Moe Levy decided to step down as executive director of the Friends, though the press mistakenly reported that Gail was resigning as national campaign chair. This confusion led to a heartfelt, if incorrect, *Winnipeg Free Press* editorial on September 8, 2010, about Gail's role in making the museum a reality, appropriately entitled "Thank You, Gail Asper." The facts were wrong, but not the sentiment:

Gail Asper has been called indefatigable but even that sells her short. Indeed, without her headlong, hell-bent-for-leather drive to bring her father's dream to life, there would be no national museum for human rights growing up at The Forks right now. But like toddlers and teenagers, this animated work of art and love is destined to leave home, so to speak. The

147

148

fundraising foundation that has raised the private cash to build the museum is going national. Ms. Asper steps down as chair of the Friends of the Canadian Museum for Human Rights as new leaders and 16 additional directors, from outside Manitoba, are appointed. The expansion will give the museum's call for cash a higher profile, and should invoke a broader sense of ownership across Canada for this expensive, unique project: It is the first national museum to be built outside Ottawa. Ms. Asper was a natural for this daunting job. With a robust personality, she possesses a mongoose's tenacity and an artist's heart. Schooled in law, Ms. Asper has made a career out of raising and giving away money for worthy works—she was central to the lobbying efforts that doubled the City of Winnipeg arts funding and sparked the matching grants program of the two higher levels of government. That casts some light on how a project that began in the $125-million range has grown to its lofty $310-million tab (at last count) once the arresting glass-and-spire design was handed from architect to engineer. More than $113 million of the $150-million target has been raised privately to date by The Friends, under Ms. Asper's leadership … There is no other museum for human rights of this scale in the world. A Canadian with an international voice should pick up the fundraising torch. Ms. Asper

deserves much gratitude, as Winnipeggers well know. In time, all Canadians will come to see that.

True enough. Yet, the key problem faced by Gail Asper, Stuart Murray, and everyone else connected with the project was another huge jump in the capital costs of the museum. Those costs had increased in 2009 from $265 million to $311 million, and now they rose again, to $351 million. This placed an enormous burden on fundraisers, who had to adjust their target from $150 million to $200 million. The battle for funding had several ramifications.

The chair of the museum's board, Arni Thorsteinson, was naturally troubled by these developments. He had already experienced several trying years. "It was a very difficult project," he recalls. "I knew the construction and financing would be difficult. I didn't quite anticipate the complexity and the difficulty of the exhibitions and what we were going to present." Another concern was the loss of Judith LaRocque, the deputy minister of Canadian heritage, who had been involved in the project almost from the beginning. In November 2010, she was appointed Canada's new ambassador and permanent representative to the Organisation for Economic Co-operation and Development, in Paris. "She deserved that appointment," says Thorsteinson, "and it showed the high esteem the government held her in. But it took away the most knowledgeable person in Ottawa who had shepherded the project for a long time."

By 2011, the situation, in Thorsteinson's view, had become worse. "We had inadequate financing," he says. "We were under siege over the contents. And I was probably spending 25 to 30 per cent of my time on the museum. As CEO of a very large business [Shelter Canadian Properties], I just didn't have that much time to spare, and there was no end in sight."

In truth, the government was in a tricky position. The museum board argued and pleaded with officials at the Department of Canadian Heritage that a $351-million building could not sit empty. Nonetheless, Thorsteinson and others were repeatedly informed that because of the Harper government's austerity program, no future funding was possible. When it was suggested to Thorsteinson that the museum opening might have to be delayed until 2017— which would have been "a terrible mistake," he says—he decided to resign his position on the board when his term was up at the end of 2011. He rejoined the Friends' board to continue to raise funds for the museum and was replaced as chair

of the CMHR Board of Trustees by vice-chair Eric Hughes, a close friend of Stephen Harper.

As of 2014, apart from Hughes, Lisa Pankratz, and Gail Asper, the CMHR board consisted of John Young, an associate professor of political science at the University of Northern British Columbia, who is vice-chair; J. Pauline Rafferty, an archaeologist and the former CEO of the Royal B.C. Museum, a position she held from 2001 to 2012; Wilton Littlechild, a lawyer who has spent more than thirty years working to build bridges between Aboriginal and non-Aboriginal people through athletics, politics, and law; Lindy Ledohowski, an adjunct research faculty member of Carleton University, who has written about Ukrainian Canadian identity politics in post-multicultural Canada; Anthony Dale of Toronto, the president and CEO of the Ontario Hospital Association, where he formerly served as vice-president of policy and public affairs; and Deena Spiro, an interior designer by profession who has served as the director of issues management for the Minister of Canadian Heritage and Official Languages.

As a chartered accountant and oil executive, Eric Hughes brought a lot of budget experience to the table at time when the museum needed that the most. In January 2012, the main issue was this: the museum now cost $86 million more than it did two years earlier; the three levels of government refused to consider additional contributions; and raising money from the private sector, especially outside Manitoba, was as challenging as ever. The Friends' chair, John Stefaniuk, and Gail Asper were defiant. "No one said it would be easy," they wrote in an e-mail to the museum's supporters. "Whatever the challenges are, we are 100 per cent committed to getting the Canadian Museum for Human Rights opened so it can begin its important work of making our country and this world a more peaceful and respectful place for all." Fair enough, yet this financial truth still raised the possibility that although the museum building would be completed on schedule, there would not be enough money to construct its exhibits. And any suggestion of enhanced government support literally drove the museum's many critics crazy.

There has not been a large government or private building project constructed in Canada in the past three decades that has not gone over budget; the Museum of Civilization in Hull, Quebec, for instance was budgeted in 1982 as costing $80 million and wound up being $340 million by the time it opened seven years later. Yet, the CMHR was held by politicians and the public to a different standard, mainly because doubts continued to be raised by a minority of people who regarded the project as a boondoggle.

The *Winnipeg Free Press* editorial board wondered about the Harper government's commitment to the project; many of its readers did not. Declared an editorial of December 23, 2011:

> The Harper government appears to have fallen out of love with the Canadian Museum for Human Rights, but it can't abandon its responsibilities that easily. The Conservatives entered into this marriage willingly and with full knowledge that complex projects inevitably run over budget … The overruns are partly related to unanticipated construction problems, including unstable bedrock where the piles were installed, and the constantly rising cost of the technologies that will be used inside the museum. These overruns are no one's fault and were to be expected in this unprecedented, one-of-a-kind project that has never been attempted anywhere in the world. The building alone has been described as the most complex construction project in North America. But it could take the Friends four or five years to raise the final $60 million, meaning it could be 2016 before the doors open. The costs of maintaining an empty building and its staff are not cheap, either. The fact is it is Mr. Harper's responsibility to finish the museum by providing the last $41 million. It's Canada's museum and his reputation that are at risk, not the Asper family's, as some backbiters like to claim. It also seems wrong that Ottawa won't even offer bridge

financing to allow the museum to open on schedule in 2013. The operating grant of $22 million a year is also on the low side compared to other national museums with a lesser purpose…The human rights museum deserves special consideration because it will be a Canadian icon, a bricks-and-mortar representation of Canada's defining values. It is not simply a museum, but an educational institution—a university, if you like—that is committed to elevating humanity one person at a time. It's a place where people will be motivated to do better and to engage in current events, to be better citizens, to get out and vote.

Some Winnipeggers were not impressed by the ongoing fiasco. "As the construction of the human rights museum lurches forward and the exterior curtain walls are installed, I am beginning to see the remarkable resemblance to a gigantic white elephant," wrote *Winnipeg Free Press* reader Terry Watkinson in a typical critical letter: "Congratulations to everyone involved. And don't worry; we taxpayers will pick up the tab as usual. Just don't ask us to go there." David King felt the same way:

It's clear to me, and to any sensible person, that if allowed to continue, this monstrosity will be an albatross around Winnipeg's neck forever. It can never make money. It will cost thousands of dollars to maintain—thousands that they cannot hope to cover with normal admissions and special events. Sure, a lot of Winnipeggers will go to see it once and perhaps take visitors to it occasionally, but not very many tourists would put Winnipeg on their must-visit list just because of the CMHR. Sadly, at this point it probably won't happen, but the best possible thing that could be done with the CMHR now would be to tear it down, recover what we can by selling the material for scrap, and turn the land into a nice park that all Winnipeggers could enjoy.

Reader Gary Hook, however, was much more positive and appreciated the newspaper's pro-museum position. "What a great editorial," he wrote in a letter to the editor published on December 30. "I have been somewhat ambivalent toward the Canadian Museum for Human Rights over the years. I was always impressed with the passion of the Aspers to build this legacy but the idea never resonated within; after reading through the editorial's logic, however, I get it. Not only do I get it, but the whole concept is exciting. What huge potential to create not only an educational institution but to develop processes and curricula to embed the learning within our national school system."

After more than a month of further commentary and a slew of letters, Gail Asper finally responded with two letters to the editor of her own. On January 24, 2012, she offered this thought: "I'm sure my father, Israel Asper, would have found the continuing discussions for and against the Canadian Museum for Human Rights to be fascinating.

"For my part, all I can say is, hey, at least it's given the detractors something to complain about besides our weather."

A week later, following another letter from reader Joe Segal implying that Izzy Asper's original intention had been to build a Holocaust museum, she wrote a lengthier rebuttal: "While many issues regarding the Canadian Museum for Human Rights are open to legitimate debate, I want to note for the record that Joe Segal is mistaken when he writes that the idea of the museum began when my father, Izzy Asper, and others 'thought of building a Holocaust museum.' As someone who was there at the very first conversation about the museum, I can assure Segal that this is totally inaccurate. Had my father wanted to build a Holocaust museum, he could have taken the $22 million that our family has invested in this project (roughly equal to what the City of Winnipeg is putting in) and[,] in the year 2000, built an extremely large stand-alone Holocaust centre in Ottawa or Winnipeg that would have been supported by those who are interested strictly in Holocaust education. My father was profoundly interested in educating Canadians on issues pertaining to human rights in general and in particular Canada's social history … This is a museum like no other in the world. To truly understand the entire scope of the museum and how history and current events will come together to teach, engage and inspire, I will invite Segal to be my guest when it opens."

Inevitably, Gail's letter triggered another round of pro-and-con replies. In a column chronicling the growth of Winnipeg and the construction of shopping centres, sports facilities, and theatres, the *Winnipeg Free Press*'s Dave O'Brien perhaps offered the most astute comment about this debate. "There are some people," he wrote on February 8, 2012, "who think society shouldn't spend a dime on art or beautiful ideas until every last pothole has been fixed and poverty eliminated, but if they had run the community over the last 100 years, there wouldn't be a symphony or a ballet, a historic park at The Forks, a new arena or anything that contributes to the higher purposes of civic life. A Winnipegger by the name of Izzy Asper had a vision for a national institution that would educate students and others about human rights. As corny as it sounds, he wanted to make a difference, not just for Winnipeg, but for the world. Some critics, particularly members of the Toronto elite, said it would never happen, but there it is, rising at The Forks in defiance of the odds and the naysayers. It will eventually be recognized as one of the country's most

beautiful buildings, but typically, some Winnipeggers would prefer it be built somewhere else, or not at all. They're the same people who opposed the construction of new athletic facilities and the wonderful pedestrian bridge over the Red River."

After several more months of haggling, the federal and Manitoba governments solved the financing conundrum. "We had Price Waterhouse confirm that our scheduling budgets were sound, but it was predicated on a 2014 opening," says Stuart Murray. The federal government finally agreed to provide the CMHR with an interest-free advance of $35 million that will start to be repaid in 2018 through anticipated revenues from programming and memberships and by using a portion of the annual $21.7 million operating funds the museum receives from the government. Likewise, the Province of Manitoba has provided the Friends with $35 million in loan guarantees, to be paid back over the next years at a low interest rate.

Despite their reluctance to step forward and solve this problem, the two governments had no choice other than to leave the completed museum empty. This arrangement, which was finalized in mid-July 2012, was "a great break for us," said Stuart Murray. "The bottom line," he told the *Toronto Star,* "is that this allows us to open in 2014."

As of September 2014, the Friends has raised $146 million from 7,800 donors, and there is no stopping Gail Asper and the rest of the organization from reaching their $150-million goal.

09

A GALLERY GUIDE

We're building an icon because it's about creating something that hasn't existed before.
RALPH APPELBAUM, 2007

WHEN ASPER FOUNDATION executive director Moe Levy was planning the Canadian Museum for Human Rights, he quickly realized that there had never been another institution of its type and size built anywhere in the world, and that there was no available guide about how to do it. In the process of recruiting the best of the available expert advisors, Levy went to see New York's Ralph Appelbaum, who heads the largest consulting firm for museum content in the United States, Ralph Appelbaum Associates (RAA). "What would be the driving element in planning the exhibits so that visitors would be moved by the exhibits to receive the key message?" Levy asked Appelbaum. "And how can you sum up the character of the message you want to leave behind?" Without a moment's hesitation Appelbaum shot back: "I can tell you in two words: moral clarity." They shook on it. A museum was born.

As Appelbaum pointed out in a January 2000 interview with *Interiors* magazine, he has consistently aimed in much of his work to create what he calls "searing moments of clarity," urging the viewers of his exhibits, however subliminally, to be kinder to their fellow humans. And that is what his intentions always have been with the CMHR. "I think of the museum's contents as 'interior architecture' that extends the story," he says. "It's the act of controlling a few hours of someone's time and setting them up to receive knowledge and certain essential experiences."

The master planner was backed up by a cadre of 140 architects, designers, and content experts back at his headquarters in New York. Over the past four decades, RAA has completed four hundred commissions in the fields of social, cultural, and natural history, and built 150 museums as well as heritage projects in a dozen countries. Apart from the CMHR, one of Appelbaum's most acclaimed assignments, completed in 1993, is the United States Holocaust Memorial Museum in Washington, D.C.,

one highlight of which is a stark mound of discarded shoes belonging to the concentration camp victims. The museum has become one of the world's most-visited, and provides a fitting tribute to one of history's most-reviled events.

Born in 1942, Appelbaum grew up in the Williamsburg neighbourhood of Brooklyn. As a child, he had a keen interest in constructing model boats and planes. He studied industrial design at Brooklyn's Pratt Institute. When he was in his early twenties, he joined the Peace Corps and was dispatched to Peru to assist with design issues. "I was given a Land Rover and told to go find people who make stuff and help them get it to the coast," he has recalled. "I met Indians who took their ceramics, strapped them to a mule, and had half-breakage. I taught them to pack their pottery in popcorn so it wouldn't break." Upon his return to New York, he worked with industrial designer Raymond Loewy before starting RAA in 1978.

At the time, most museums were essentially staid spaces, displaying unimaginative exhibits, but Appelbaum thought of a museum as an interactive, technological wonder, a place where patrons could have a genuine out-of-body experience—or close to it. Peter Prichard, the chairman of the highly original Newseum in Washington, D.C., designed by RAA, has called Appelbaum a visionary. Appelbaum convinced Prichard and his team that a media museum could appeal to journalists and poets, as well as to the public. In December 2009, London's *Sunday Times* rated the Newseum as one of the "world's 12 coolest museums."

At the heart of any museum, Appelbaum told the *New York Times* in April 1999, is sharing. Museums have to be "inter-generationally friendly; they don't bring objects together, they bring people together." A decade later he has not changed his mind on this point. Appelbaum still claims that museums can be as accessible as nightly news reports and keep patrons up to date. "That gives us an enormous capability to be relevant and current. The modern museum is a lively gathering point."

"Museums," he maintains, "are places where you discover the authentic, as opposed to alternate venues where you indulge in fictional pleasures, mainly for entertainment. This is one of the pleasures of the Museum for Human Rights. It puts you in an immediate relationship with filmmakers and writers, with poets and theatre professionals. Show biz is not new to the museum world. Some of the grandest and greatest museums have a pretty terrific sense of showmanship. A visit to the Louvre in Paris, or to Bilbao in Spain, or the Uffizi Gallery in Florence, provides different vistas of magnificent showmanship."

Not so long ago, the media competed for people's discretionary income; now time has become their most valuable currency, particularly since it is ultimate and finite. "Museums can bring families together in a creative environment where they can share the most practical ideas about how to live together," he says.

Museums, Appelbaum points out, have an austere and exclusive history. "The DNA of most museums does not come out of a democratic tradition," he notes. "They were places where only select connoisseurs felt comfortable. But museums today try to address everyone. You can spend far longer than you could at a ninety-minute movie, enjoy a meal, view fabulous architecture, great panoramas of your city, and, most of the time, a constant diet of changing, revealing exhibitions."

Human rights, like museums, are concerned about every aspect of existence. They showcase how we come to terms with the social world, and awaken our common humanity, our sense of justice and partnership. In Appelbaum's view, the CMHR in one way resembles "a giant onion with sets of layers that visitors keep peeling away to reveal deeper and more specialized levels of information. Its first goal is to make people receptive, to get them to relax and enjoy a multi-hour journey through the way people thought, and how they'll think in the future."

By design, the CMHR's galleries offer a wide variety of techniques—physical, emotional, intellectual, visual, auditory, and kinesthetic. Each of those approaches appeals to people's senses, making it easy to enter into the storytelling—and listening—mode. "We want to seize the visitors' attention," says Appelbaum. "And we want them to realize that in them is the capability to do good and to be special, to be similar to the exemplars that we see all around the museum."

There are several ways you can enter the CMHR: through a legal portal, through the Charter of Rights and Freedoms, or through an individual's story. The museum's objective is to present the extraordinary human rights struggles in Canada and around the world by courageous individuals who have dared to speak out, to correct injustices, and to halt abuse. "Our goal is to have visitors remember those documents and storytellers—not allow their messages to slide past, but to remember how they made us feel," Appelbaum adds. "That kind of sharing builds a community of people who have

157

been sensitized to doing good, sharing the kind of information which is at the heart of any ethical project. This is a project rooted in the highest levels of ethics and values."

APPELBAUM DELIBERATELY chose not to use the standard tools of a museum when he conceived the exhibits for the CMHR. Instead, he created a multi-sensory experience using cutting-edge technology and Canadian talent to produce the museum's films, living theatre, and storytellers. "What we really have here," says Appelbaum, "are trained, professional actors who will help bring alive some of the events that happened to people who didn't leave a clear record. Within the museum, visitors will discover the first glimmers of issues before they become codified. This is the place where people come to share their experiences, not dry theories. All of these elements are meant to be orchestrated seamlessly with movement through the unusual architecture.

"One of the great experiences here," he continues, "is that visitors can go to a concierge's desk and say something like, 'I want to be part of the community and people who care about other people. What do I do? Who should I ask?' And we'll provide them with solid connections and information—websites and people to talk to. That's the strength of this museum. It's not a place where you go and say, 'Wow, I saw wonderful things. Now I can go away and do something else.' People will leave the magic tower with the experience sticking in their minds. They will not get some of the stories they heard out of their minds—or the look in the storyteller's eyes out of their memories. When they hear about people who were abused, . . . it will encourage them to watch the television news with a more refined eye, [and] spot those danger signs that can lead to the loss of human rights."

Above all, the CMHR is what Appelbaum calls "a place of ideas" rather than a museum of objects. "Most people think of museums

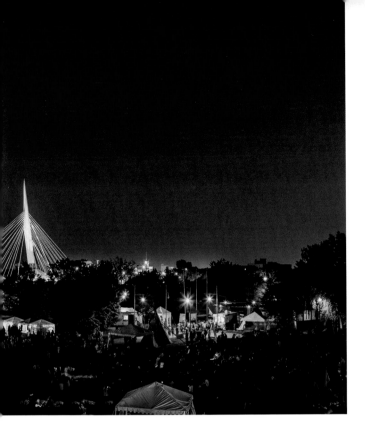

facing Celebrating Aboriginal Day 2013 and the birth of the CMHR.

describes as "enormous architectural roots," which begin the process of making each visitor aware of their responsibilities as a member of society. "It does this," he adds, "by giving you a set of increasingly powerful encounters with media until you reach a point about midway in the museum where all of a sudden you become a subject of the museum yourself. Suddenly, it's about you, and about how you will find a way to activate your own sense of moral outrage churning within your soul. What you do with those feelings, and how in Canadian society you can find an avenue to become engaged. That doesn't mean you must go out and join an organization. It may very well mean you are nicer to people when you leave the museum. Because what counts is human kindness, compassion, tolerance, and human empathy: that you simply treat people the way you want to be treated."

159

as being about things," he says. "But this is a museum meant to release in the visitors a sense of their latent goodness. We want to sensitize them to what it's like not to have human rights— and make them sensitive to the importance of being good to others. It's actually rather a simple goal supported by every religion since the beginning of time: to love thy neighbour. And yet we've lived through times in human history when we've treated people dreadfully, and still do. Our kids still come home from playgrounds having been bullied. We still read and watch horrid news events that we can't explain. This museum will make visitors sensitive to those feel-bad occurrences and help in the formulation and sponsorship of policies that can really make a difference."

THE CMHR EXPERIENCE is a journey both figuratively and literally. It is a long walk, not a luxurious stroll. That experience begins by walking in under the building through what Appelbaum

Visitors are immediately immersed in a multi-sensory human rights experience the moment they enter the physically dramatic surroundings of the introductory gallery What Are Human Rights? and its remarkable "object theatre," a large media installation. An undulating timeline presents a sweeping survey of human rights concepts throughout history and around the world.

Aboriginal concepts of humanity are the focus of one of the most dramatic spaces in the museum. The Indigenous Perspectives gallery includes a spectacular work of art, a 360-degree film, and a circular theatre made

160

of curved wood panels representing the multitude of Canadian indigenous communities. An outdoor terrace incorporates local plants and accommodates ceremonial smudging and other activities.

The locally produced film narrates the story of Canada's indigenous peoples from their perspective. "The film is a positive articulation of indigenous peoples' concepts of humanity and responsibilities to each other and the land," says Stuart Murray. For the theatre's wood panels, the museum asked Aboriginal artists to consult with youth groups and then carve their personal representation of human rights onto a wooden panel. Here, too, on display is "Trace," the very large and unique hand-pressed clay "beads" created by Rebecca Belmore, the Winnipeg-based Anishinaabe artist, with the assistance of thousands of young volunteers. "The clay she is using," says Murray, "comes from Manitoba. And there is a strong connection to the land and the importance of treaties. She hopes that someday the young people who made the beads will return to the museum with their own children."

In the CMHR's largest gallery, Canadian Journeys, it is Canada's human rights journey that forms the central narrative. This gallery takes a multi-layered approach to dozens of Canadian human rights stories—from French-language rights to the Chinese head tax, from same-sex marriage to cultural dispossession in the North. A two-storey-high digital canvas tells human rights stories; other stories are explored in a video theatre, story niches, and activity areas. Visitors, for instance, not only will learn about the Canadian link to the Underground Railway and the escape of American slaves north to freedom, they also will feel like they are on this dangerous and life-altering journey with them.

Legal aspects of Canadian human rights, including Canada's Charter of Rights and Freedoms, and their evolution, are examined in the Protecting Rights in Canada gallery. An ambient "living tree" projection evokes the constant adaptation of Canadian laws to social change. And a digitally interfaced debate table enables visitors to explore pivotal court cases from various perspectives.

Examining the Holocaust is a gallery that educates visitors about the importance of defending human rights, asking how and why such horror could occur. Touch-screen monitors allow visitors to analyze techniques used by the Nazis in the genocide conducted against European Jews and to see how similar methods have been used in other genocides.

One of the key features in the middle of this gallery is an installation of glass shards designed to give visitors "a very uncomfortable feeling," as Stuart Murray explains. It is a strong reference to Kristallnacht, the infamous Night of Broken Glass that took place throughout Nazi Germany in November 1938. Adds Clint Curle, a former CMHR researcher and now the head of stakeholder relations, Appelbaum's intention with the glass shard installation "was to

illustrate the fragility of human rights and how easily they can be destroyed and obliterated, even in a democracy."

Around the Holocaust gallery's perimeter are three thematic walls that focus on the abuse of state power, the oppression of minority groups, and the relationship of war and genocide. To connect these complex macro themes with the micro themes, individual stories are deployed to resonate with visitors in a way that recalls a scrapbook design. Panels are layered on top of panels to bring home the message, as Curle says, "that the museum can only offer a snippet of the millions of Holocaust stories that could be told." Along the perimeter walls, Appelbaum has also included a series of drawers that visitors can open. Inside each drawer are artifacts that can be held and examined, and that offer another intimate connection to the human experience of the Holocaust. The gallery's "emotional anchor," according to Curle, is a large glass case enclosing a massive map of the Auschwitz-Birkenau concentration and death camp, and juxtaposed

with a small collection of artifacts that link the tragedy with Holocaust's perpetrators, bystanders, and victims. This gallery also emphasizes understanding the Holocaust from a Canadian perspective and confronts anti-Semitism within Canadian history.

The power of hope and hard work is showcased in Turning Points for Humanity, a gallery that presents and explores the Universal Declaration of Human Rights (UDHR), including the role of Canadian John Peters Humphrey, who wrote the original draft of the UDHR. The gallery also considers how grassroots movements have expanded the concept of human rights. Large digital monitors relay the power of activism and examine children's rights, women's rights, and disability rights, as well as other important issues.

Gross human rights violations are the dominant theme of Breaking the Silence, a series of exhibits that explore the role of secrecy and denial in global atrocities. These exhibits present many genocide stories but focus on those

genocides officially recognized by Canada and other countries: the Ukrainian Holodomor, the Armenian genocide, the Holocaust, the Rwandan genocide, and the Srebrenica genocide of the Bosnian War.

A youth-oriented gallery, Actions Count, is a space where visitors can experience the connection between individual actions and collective human rights, and learn about Canadians who have worked to make a difference in this arena. This gallery includes an interactive table where visitors can make individual choices in situations ranging from bullying to challenging inequality and discrimination, and thereby understand the impact of those individual choices.

In the Rights Today gallery, visitors are brought face to face with contemporary human rights struggles and activism. Through everyday objects, an interactive wall map of ongoing global issues, a tapestry of human rights defenders, and a theatre that teaches media literacy, the connection between individuals and collective human rights is explored and leads naturally into the next gallery, Inspiring Change. This gallery is intended to spark personal commitment to positive social change, and asks visitors to contribute their voices by leaving messages for others.

In the final gallery, visitors move into a place where they *can* take action: a place where they can talk to experts, pick up a brochure, or visit

a website. They can take a journey up into the Israel Asper Tower of Hope, look out over the city, and ponder their experience in the CMHR before entering a slow elevator that takes them down to the Stuart Clark Garden of Contemplation—where they can sit and think some more—before they proceed to the final ramp that takes them back to the Bonnie and John Buhler Hall. From there visitors might choose to see a film or one of the CMHR's temporary exhibits, have a meal, or walk the grounds. At the end of this journey, too, is the remarkable story of how this museum was built, which includes an electronic donor wall and videos of key donors showcasing the reasons they chose to participate in the CMHR.

RALPH APPELBAUM believes that a museum for human rights could only have happened in a democracy like Canada. "It represents a country that cares about the weakest and not just the strongest," he says. "And for Canada to do this is one of the most courageous acts of museum making. It's not courageous to build an art museum. You just have to take good care of the art. It's precious and it's glorious. But one doesn't have to build a museum for human rights. It has to come from some deeper need and more profound desire within the national body to want to do this—not only for ourselves but . . . for others. That's a great gift."

AFTERWORD

AS ONE OF THE WORLD'S newest museums, it's appropriate that the Canadian Museum for Human Rights should perpetuate the oldest of its discipline's traditions. The classic Greek word *mouseion* ("museum" is its Latin derivative) roughly translates into "a seat of the muses"— a place where original thought can bubble up into social and political agendas. Unlike most museums, which merely preserve and display the material aspects of heritage, this unusual Winnipeg-based "lighthouse" will be an activist institution of learning, dedicated to righting the wrongs in human relations.

Walking through its twisting corridors, visitors will find it to be a place of solace and healing, its operations based on two approaches. The first of these is to create a learning environment, with lively lectures and exhibits that capture mind and heart, larded with storytelling and panache. The second face of this high-tech, imaginatively outfitted institution is hands-on activism. Its dedication is stunning, but its success will be judged by its purpose of reducing inhumanity among people. Most museums pride themselves on being the memory of humankind; this one will make history instead of merely storing it.

A subsidiary purpose of the CMHR will be to introduce new sets of heroic personages to Canadians. Don Cherry will have to share his populist glory with bunches of "no-names" like Viola Desmond, the black Halifax business-woman who in 1946 refused to use the balcony seats of a movie house specifically reserved for patrons of colour. After she wouldn't move, she was found guilty of not paying the one-cent difference in tax on the balcony ticket from the main-floor theatre. It was six and a half decades until Viola Desmond was granted a posthumous pardon by the Government of Nova Scotia, in 2010. The exhibits of the Canadian Museum for Human Rights will introduce a new gallery of role models such as Viola Desmond, Louise McKinney, Emily Murphy,

Henrietta Edwards, and Irene Parlby, as well as better-known heroes such as General Roméo Dallaire, Nelson Mandela, Tecumseh, Nellie McClung, and so many others.

They will get their due, but so must the others who abandoned their job descriptions by treating this museum-building endeavour not as a job, or even as a calling, but more like a personal crusade. The list of activists is headed by the duo of Gail Asper and Moe Levy, who came perilously close to having the politicians they mercilessly lobbied agree (though never out loud) that they would approve the damn thing, if only Moe and Gail promised to vamoose.

The Asper Foundation's executive director Moe Levy spent five years camped in the Château Laurier hotel explaining why building the CMHR was not negotiable. "Look," he told a group of doubters during the construction phase, "Winnipeg has one shot at doing something really remarkable—truly world scale. What we're building at the Forks is something that's not being done anywhere in the world, because it's so difficult to do. Going in, we knew this had to be the very best." And it is.

Izzy Asper's daughter, Gail, set new standards in tenacity, exhibiting a combination of irresistible charm, feline mischief, and a remarkable version of life force that explains why Jewish mothers consider their offspring fully formed only when they graduate from medical school. Her record of raising

$143 million (as of spring 2014) is unmatched, and she managed to do so while keeping her sense of humanity and humour. Well, as long as you wrote the cheque. Charles Coffey, then in charge of the Royal Bank's Manitoba operations and an ardent supporter, came up with the brilliant notion that if the Gail-Moe duo couldn't make the case for the museum strong enough to turn the tide, they ought to set up a professional advisory council that could. They did, and chief advisor Arni Thorsteinson, as well as Coffey, became indispensable. Manitoba premier Gary Doer became a dedicated supporter, as did Winnipeg mayors Glen Murray and Sam Katz.

As well, through the darkest days, David and Leonard Asper willingly continued to endorse the Asper Foundation's promotion of the project, agreeing to sink millions of dollars into its development, and used every connection they had to secure government support.

Finally, the project would never have got off the ground if it had not been for Prime Minister Jean Chrétien's initial support and funding, making possible the inaugural announcement at the Forks on April 17, 2003. Later, and most important, Prime Minister Stephen Harper took over the file and fulfilled all of his generous promises.

SITTING AT THE crossroads of Canada—the historic Forks site, where two great riverbeds meet and Aboriginal leaders once negotiated peace treaties—the CMHR celebrates how far we have come in the respect we have for one another, and reminds us how much further we have yet to go. A lighthouse analogy is a good one, since it signals both lurking dangers and the safety inherent in such safe-haven values as equality, respect, and responsibility. There is no quick fix. But the small triumphs and large miracles that have come together here to make this unlikely haven possible in the most unlikely of locations teach a lesson: nothing is impossible if you want it badly enough and are willing to invest your energies and passions in its realization.

This book is being published while most of the CMHR's dedicated founders are still alive and willing to reconstruct the details of its creation. The Canadian Museum for Human Rights will quickly grow into an essential, animating agency that deals in the covenants that regulate, inhibit, or encourage the evolution of human rights in a world caught up in the suddenly barely controllable acceleration of history. It is dedicated to improving individual and collective opportunities in the exercise of basic rights, moral imperatives, and civil liberties. That's a tall order. But then, its guiding light is a tall tower.

THERE ARE TWO glaring absences in the lineup of dedicated idealists who gave life to this startling museum. They are, of course, Izzy and Babs Asper. Izzy, who was the museum's founding spirit and initial guiding light, died of a heart attack in October 2003, before its design was chosen or construction was started.

And Babs, who passed away in July 2011, was his lifelong partner who dedicated her last years to making the museum a reality. It was at the St-Boniface Hospital, in the same room where their father's body was lying, that Izzy and Babs's two sons and daughter pledged they would get the museum built. "We decided that the real harm would be in not trying," said Gail as she recalled that tragic occasion.

Their late father's intentions were set out in his memorable interview with Evan Solomon: "Unless I can do this well, I won't do it," said Izzy, who paused, then added as a kind of closing benediction, "When people come to this museum, no matter how well-versed they are in the subject, they will leave with their lives changed. Canadians tend to aim for the middle. Here, we're reaching for the stars."

Babs's involvement went well beyond fundraising and moral support. She was a guardian of setting quality standards in the museum's design and authenticity in its execution. "It

must be a very high-quality building with a very high-quality message delivered in the most honest and intelligent way possible" was her credo. "This will take very careful thinkers who understand the subjects they are dealing with. It has to be absolutely authentic. Somebody who says they know the subject of human rights peripherally is not enough. They must have experienced it first-hand—and have the intelligence to express it in the museum forum. For this project to be successful people will have to be moved by their visits; their views will have to be changed; they will think differently. You don't want people to just come and go and say, 'So what?' It has to have some emotional impact, even if they just take away one thing: a genuine feeling of profound remorse for the

abuse of human rights, so prominent in our histories."

"The subject of the building, really its genesis, was the Durban Conference in 2001 that turned into such a debacle of racism," she liked to remind visitors. "It was supposed to be against racism but turned into a racist conference, particularly anti-Israel and anti-Semitic. Izzy felt that the young people in Canada were not getting a proper education in real human rights and anti-racism. So we started the course, just one class; one small group from a Jewish school in Winnipeg. We put together a course where the young people studied human rights and racism for eight weeks and then went to the Holocaust Museum in Washington and several other human rights monuments and education

institutions in Washington, because there was really nothing comparable to take them to in Canada. There was no other place to take them in Canada that would have any impact."

Babs took on the museum as a personal crusade: to develop an understanding of what human rights are and what oppressed people experience when their rights are denied. "The other thing is to be proactive," she insisted. "This is definitely the most important part of the museum, ... to be proactive in protecting and promoting human rights and to see and recognize when human rights—whether it's in

schools or governments—are being violated." Babs died before the building was completed but had visited the construction site almost daily. "Every time I see the museum I just get very choked up because it is really an incredible building," she noted with pride. "It's going to be an amazing institution. This is Izzy's final legacy to Winnipeg. It's a tribute to his vision and his determination and subsequently a tribute to Gail's vision and Moe's determination." And Babs's enduring and, yes, loving dedication.

Most museums celebrate the past. This one will change the future.